The Adventure of Difference

PARALLAX  RE-VISIONS OF CULTURE AND SOCIETY

Stephen G. Nichols, Gerald Prince, and Wendy Steiner,
Series Editors

The Adventure of Difference

Philosophy after Nietzsche and Heidegger

Gianni Vattimo

Translated by Cyprian Blamires
with the assistance of Thomas Harrison

The Johns Hopkins University Press
Baltimore

Copyright © Aldo Garzanti Editore 1980
This English translation copyright © Polity Press 1993
Printed in Great Britain

First published in the United States of America in 1993 by
The Johns Hopkins University Press
2715 North Charles Street
Baltimore, Maryland 21218–4319

Library of Congress Cataloging-in-Publication Data
Vattimo, Gianni, 1936–
    [Avventure della differenza. English]
    The adventure of difference : philosophy after Nietzsche and
Heidegger / Gianni Vattimo : translated by Cyprian Blamires with the
assistance of Thomas Harrison.
        p.   cm. — (Parallax)
    Includes bibliographical references.
    ISBN 0–8018–4643–9 (alk. paper)
    1. Difference (Philosophy)   2. Heidegger, Martin, 1889–1976.
3. Nietzsche, Friedrich Wilhelm, 1844–1900. I. Title. II. Series:
Parallax (Baltimore, Md.)
B3654.V383A9813   1993
190′.9′04—dc20   92–40885
                                                             CIP

A catalog record for this book is available from the British Library.

Contents

Acknowledgements

The author and publishers wish to thank the following for permission to use copyright material.

George Weidenfeld & Nicolson Ltd and Random House, Inc. for material from Friedrich Nietzsche, *The Will to Power*, trans. W. Kaufmann and R. J. Hollingdale. Copyright © 1967 by Walter Kaufmann.

Every effort has been made to trace all the copyright holders, but if any have been inadvertently overlooked the publishers will be pleased to make the necessary arrangement at the first opportunity.

Abbreviations

From time to time, references in the text or notes are in the form of (bracketed) abbreviations. These references are all to works by Nietzsche or Heidegger, and the key to the abbreviations is as follows:

Works by Nietzsche

HATH   *Human, all too Human*, translated by R. J. Hollingdale, Cambridge, 1986.

UM II   *Untimely Meditations*, Part II, translated by R. J. Hollingdale, Cambridge, 1983.

WP   *The Will to Power*, translated by W. Kaufmann and R. J. Hollingdale, New York and London, 1968.

Works by Heidegger

BT   *Being and Time*, translated by J. Macquarrie and E. Robinson, Oxford, 1962.

BW   *Basic Writings*, edited by D. F. Krell, New York, 1977.

EP   *The End of Philosophy*, translated by J. Stambaugh, New York, 1973.

ER   *The Essence of Reasons*, translated by T. Malick, Evanston, 1969.

ID   *Identity and Difference*, translated by J. Stambaugh, New York, 1969.

LH   'Letter on Humanism', translated by F. A. Capuzzi and J. Glenn Gray, in *Basic Writings*, pp. 193–242.

N   *Nietzsche*, 2 vols, Pfullingen, 1962 (references to the German edition).

PLT   *Poetry, Language, Thought*, translated by A. Hofstadter, New York, 1975.

QT   *The Question concerning Technology and other Essays*, translated by W. Lovitt, New York, 1977.

SVG   *Der Satz vom Grund*, Pfullingen, 1957 (citations trans-

TB   lated by C. P. Blamires).

      On Time and Being, translated by J. Stambaugh, New

WT   York, 1972.

      What is called Thinking? translated by J. Glenn Gray, New York, 1968.

Introduction

THE common thread in this somewhat heterogeneous collection of essays, all dating from the 1970s, is the idea of *difference*. If there seems to be more than a hint of inconsistency in the varying approaches adopted to this topic, the reason is to be found in what Hegel called 'the thing itself', i.e. not simply the 'content' of my discourse – the concept of difference itself, with all its ambiguities, implications, and aporias – but the whole complex play of relations between this concept and historical experience, in other words, the 'spirit of the age'. Typical of this spirit has been the prevalence in recent years of a preoccupation with Nietzsche and Heidegger, the two writers whose ideas provide the commonest and most fundamental reference points for these essays. Nietzsche and Heidegger have been regarded by some as tending towards the same viewpoint while others have seen them as fundamentally at odds, and these contrasting responses are both reflected in the present volume, but one thing these essays all reflect is my conviction that Nietzsche and Heidegger have done more than any other thinkers currently within our cultural horizon to transform radically the whole idea of thinking, so that since them 'to think' has come to mean something different from what it meant before. With Nietzsche this is particularly evident in

1

the ideas of the death of God and the superman.[1] In the early part of this volume I take these concepts to be an original and radical reformulation of the unity of theory and practice; the new type of thinking Nietzsche is preparing for is done in the light of the eternal recurrence of the same, i.e. in the light of a unity of essence and existence, existence and meaning. This can come about only by virtue of a radical transformation of social relations, a transformation that must be internal to the individual before it can be external to him. From such a perspective, thinking as traditionally conceived and carried on looks like a 'malady', for it is marked by an (allegedly insuperable) separation between being and value, event and meaning. But according to Nietzsche, all such separation is in reality purely a function of relations of domination, or, as I have shown elsewhere,[2] of the 'Oedipal structure of time'. This does not therefore mean that the question of 'what it means to think' is purely a matter of praxis, the revolutionary transformation of social relations, for such a transformation can effectively give rise to new thinking only if at the same time there is an elimination of the structures of domination at the point where they are most deeply entrenched, namely in 'grammar'.[3] It is with the categories of grammar that we order the way we basically experience the world, which we see in terms, for example, of the relation of subject to predicates (ownership), subject to object and substance to accident. The new thinking envisaged by Nietzsche with his proclamation of the superman may also be regarded as a kind of 'adventure of difference', above all in the sense that, ridding itself of all the metaphysical timidity and defensiveness embodied in the reduction of everything to a single principle – the possession of which guarantees that nothing will happen to us – it can surrender itself to the multiplicity of appearances, appearances liberated from that Platonic condemnation which, in making them copies of a transcendent original, immediately creates hierarchies and ascesis. In his observations on Nietzsche, Heidegger saw that we cannot sidestep the force of all this by viewing it as an aesthetic reprise of the notion of play; it is rather to be seen as a rigorous expression of the ultimate *unfoundedness* and procedural *rigour* in which thinking operates in the age of technology. The existence of technological man is unquestionably a self-surrender to the play of multiplicity and appearances; but at the same time this unfounded multiplicity is ordered as a varied ensemble of formal languages, each endowed with its own precise grammar. The play is not to be understood in terms of some non-essentialness or arbitrariness but in terms of a subjection to rules that are at bottom gratuitous and unfounded.

And yet, is this really all that 'difference' means in Nietzsche? Does he view 'difference' purely and supremely as the liberation of thinking for multiplicity through a destruction of Platonic hierarchies, which finally brings the realization that God is dead? If so, there would be serious implications for the whole of Heidegger's thought, with its own much more explicit appeal to difference. This thought would be reduced to nothing more than a manifestation of permanent nostalgia for Platonism and metaphysics, insofar as it is for ever striving to grasp Being, though as event and not as stable structure, by starting from a 'same' (*das Selbe*) which, running through the history of Being, makes possible both the differences between the epochs and the dialogue between them. This is how I have sometimes presented Heidegger in the earlier essays in this volume, but those essays are still closely bound up with something I now regard as a 'dream': the dream of superhumanity as an attainable condition in which a harmonization of existence and meaning is achieved. This harmonization is the constant element underneath the various shifts and turns in these essays, but I now view it as still too much under the spell of the dialectical model. What can it in fact mean to think of the superman as the man liberated *for* the differences and the multiplicity of experience, if this liberated man continues to

3

be imagined on the model of the subject who has 'returned to himself' at the end of a wandering itinerary that still covertly follows the dialectical guidebook, a subject who has finally realized the unity of event and meaning, the 'beauty' of Hegel's *Aesthetics*, the perfect coincidence of internal and external? (This was Marcuse's dream, and it has been the dream of the most radical revolutionary thinkers past and present.) On this question, the crucial essay in the present volume is the fourth one, 'The Will to Power as Art'. There I begin to detail all the consequences that result in Nietzsche's thought from the fact that he takes art as the model for the notion of the will to power, while also describing art as the locus of the decline of the subject, of the dissolution of form, unity and hierarchies. It is this model that demonstrates the futility of continuing to interpret the superman and the will to power dialectically.

If to become liberated for difference and multiplicity also implies that we accept the disintegration of unity – with the subject unchangeably a *dividuum* and 'harmonization' therefore a dream – as paradoxically 'constitutive', then difference thus re-emerges in its Heideggerian sense which, from the point of view of the philosophy of the superman (see the third essay, 'Nietzsche and Difference'), had looked like a manifestation of residual metaphysical nostalgia. Difference re-emerges in other words as the denial and de-stitution of presence, or, in the language of my later essays, as an 'ungrounding' of any claim of presence to definitiveness. The central importance I attribute to this 'ungrounding', as is particularly evident in the essay on *Andenken*, is in no way meant to suggest a revival of a kind of existentialist vision of man as problematic or as finitude marked by the drama of choice; Nietzsche inoculated us once and for all against that sort of bombastic notion. Rather, difference as de-stitution of definitiveness from presence is essential if thinking is to constitute itself as 'critical' thinking and resist every temptation to seek a dialectical harmonization – and hence ignore

4

all proclamations of the end of alienation and the attainment of a condition of authenticity – for example, in some political order passing as 'real socialism'. Difference as ungrounding is thus a response to the call for critical thinking made by those thinkers who have lived the adventure of the dialectic most dramatically, such as Adorno. Though for the most part unspoken, he is an ever-present reference point in these essays.

Although difference as ungrounding is not principally meant to be understood as a return to existentialism, it does *also* carry the suggestion of a rediscovery of the finitude that is constitutive of existence. For, to the thinking which listens to its call, existence communicates itself as inseparably bound up with being-towards-death (in the terms that Heidegger was the first to put forward). Consequently, in the later essays in this volume, I tend to the view that the meaning of the title of Heidegger's first great work, *Being and Time*, must more and more be sought in a philosophy of 'decline', a philosophy which sees what is constitutive of Being not as the fact of its prevailing, but as the fact of its disappearing. This ontology of decline also, of course, has possible 'psychological' implications, though these do not point in the direction of a generally pessimistic vision of life. But Heidegger's thought is in reality a response to a demand felt with increasing force and clarity in modern experience, for an ontology organized in 'weak' categories. As Nietzsche had seen very clearly,[4] and as Heidegger shows in ontological terms, the metaphysical tradition is the tradition of 'violent' thinking. With its predilection for unifying, sovereign and generalizing categories, and with its cult of the *arché*, it manifests a fundamental insecurity and exaggerated self-importance from which it then reacts into over-defensiveness. All the categories of metaphysics are violent categories: Being and its attributes, the 'first' cause, man as 'responsible', and even the will to power, if that is read metaphysically as affirmation or as the assumption of power over the world. They must be 'weakened' or relieved of their

5

excess power in the sense suggested, for example, by Benjamin's talk of metropolitan man's 'distracted perception'.[5] It is in the light of such an 'ontology of decline' that Heidegger can talk of the technical world, of what he calls the *Ge-Stell* – and therefore mass society – as being also the place where the event of Being is heralded. For it is perhaps precisely at the point where the forgetting of difference appears to be most complete, in the experience of metropolitan man, that Being speaks afresh; and it does so in its 'weak' modality, which involves a dissolution of the subject with all the violent characteristics (those of master and slave, for example) attributed to him by the metaphysical tradition. It is *this* weakened subject who lives being-towards-death, rather than Kierkegaardian ethical or religious man, all too solemnly convinced that in every choice he makes his eternal destiny is at stake. The weakened subject should thus also be open to a less melodramatic relation with his own mortality. That is also the reason why I allude at a certain point in these essays to 'animality'; though this idea is certainly alien to the letter of the Heideggerian text, there seems to be a hint of it in the difference/ungrounding/mortality nexus. Through animality, as the focus for a founding/ungrounding of culture, possibilities of dialogue seem to open up between the heirs of Heidegger and other theorists of human reality, who exploit the results of the positive human sciences (biology, psychology, the 'ecology of mind') to a greater extent than Heidegger would have thought feasible or legitimate. But for the present these avenues still remain to be explored.

Notes

1 See my *Il soggetto e la maschera. Nietzsche e il problema della liberazione*, Milan, 1979.
2 Ibid., pp. 249ff.

3 'I fear we are not getting rid of God because we still believe in grammar....', Friedrich Nietzsche, *Twilight of the Idols*, trans. R. J. Hollingdale, London, 1968, p. 38.
4 At least I think this is the meaning of texts like the one in 'The Wanderer and his Shadow',

> 350: – *The golden watchword.* – Many chains have been laid upon man so that he should no longer behave like an animal: and he has in truth become gentler, more spiritual, more joyful, more reflective than any animal is. Now, however, he suffers from having worn his chains for so long, from being deprived for so long of clear air and free movement: – these chains, however, I shall never cease from repeating, are those heavy and pregnant errors contained in the conceptions of morality, religion and metaphysics. Only when this *sickness from one's chains* has also been overcome will the first great goal have truly been attained: the separation of man from the animals.
>
> F. Nietzsche, *Human, all too Human*, ed. E. Heller, trans. R. J. Hollingdale, Cambridge, 1986, p. 393.

See also the very fine concluding aphorism in the first part of *Human, all too Human*, part i, section 34; an excellent little treatise on 'the weakened subject'.
5 W. Benjamin, 'Das Kunstwerk im Zeitalter seiner technischer Reproduzierbarkeit' in *Gesammelte Schriften*, ed. R. Tiedermann and H. Schweppenhauser, Frankfurt, 1974, vol. I ch. 2, pp. 431ff.

1

Hermeneutical Reason/ Dialectical Reason

IN *Truth and Method*[1] Gadamer engages in a lengthy critical discussion of 'historical consciousness', which he considers to be a characteristic feature of the philosophical mentality of recent centuries. At several points in this discussion, he makes occasional very specific reference[2] to Nietzsche's account of the 'historical malady' in the second of the *Untimely Meditations*. To a considerable extent, Gadamer's hermeneutical ontology may in fact be viewed as a deliberate attempt to go beyond precisely that condition of the modern spirit diagnosed by Nietzsche in terms of such a malady. But Gadamer's enterprise brings a whole new dimension to the theme by making a series of connections with Heidegger's discourse on metaphysics and its overcoming.[3] It seems legitimate therefore to take a closer look at hermeneutical ontology's more or less explicit claim to stand entirely outside any such historical consciousness or 'malady'. This kind of inquiry is all the more pertinent in that many of the contemporary schools of thought that touch in one way or another on the themes of hermeneutical ontology, relying more often directly on Heidegger than on Gadamer, at the same time also claim Nietzsche as their forerunner. A debate with hermeneutical ontology on the subject of the historical malady seems likely therefore to throw light on a whole complex of interesting issues while offering a unique perspective on numerous problems of contemporary philosophy. For not only have the themes of hermeneutics aroused an ever-growing interest over a wide area of philosophy,[4] but there is concurrently a new historical-theoretical interest in the work of Nietzsche and in the seemingly intractable problems involved in its interpretation. Furthermore, on an even more radical level, Nietzsche, Heidegger and the theorists of hermeneutics are right to point out that the 'historical malady' is one of the salient features of modern consciousness, and that overcoming it is a task yet to be tackled. The reference in the title of this essay to 'dialectical reason', which is to be understood in the sense it has in Sartre's later thought,[5] alludes to a point I hope to demonstrate: that Nietzsche, leaving behind his initial approach (in *Untimely Meditations*) to the problem of overcoming the historical malady, goes on to elaborate a new approach which, far removed from hermeneutical ontology, is ultimately comparable with Sartre's dialectical reason.

There are four basic points I want to make here: first, I want to give a brief summary of the essential features of Nietzsche's definition of the historical malady; second, I want to identify the elements of the critique of historical consciousness that underlie hermeneutical ontology and to consider the alternative it proposes to that consciousness; third, I want to test this alternative against the demands that gave rise to Nietzsche's critique of the historical malady, taking into consideration the different ways in which these were expressed as Nietzsche's work developed; and finally, I want to show how Nietzsche's thought, unlike hermeneutical ontology, seems to take a dialectical turn, with apparently more impressive results.

When Nietzsche speaks of a historical *malady*,[6] his chief aim is to emphasize the fact that the excessive historiographical awareness he thinks characteristic of the nineteenth century is also and inevitably an inability to create new history. The 'historical' nature of the malady reflects both its

10

concern with historiography and its involvement with history as *res gestae* – negatively, for it amounts to an inability to generate a history of one's own, because of an obsession with the science of things past.[7]

Thus we have the well-known passages in the second part of the *Untimely Meditations*, such as the story of the disciple of Heraclitus who cannot move even a finger, so conscious is he of the vanity of every initiative that claims to *establish* anything in history, which he sees as pure passing; or there is the discussion of the forgetting involved in every historical action, a certain 'injustice' that is the opposite of all that 'objectivity' to which modern historians lay claim.[8] According to Nietzsche, that purity and naturalness of the relationship between life and history so characteristic of the tragic epoch of the Greeks was subsequently degraded *'by science, by the demand that history should be a science'*.[9]

As a rule, the Nietzschean discourse in this part of *Untimely Meditations* is (to some extent justifiably) identified with this critique of historiographical 'objectivity'; or, in other words, with a critique of the claim that the methodological ideal of the natural sciences may be applied to historiographical knowledge. It is with just this problem that Gadamer's *Truth and Method* begins, and it is clear that contemporary hermeneutics can in this sense rightly claim to be heir to the Nietzschean critique. But what I want to do here is to show that for Nietzsche this is far from being the end of the matter; since the way he goes on to develop his critique of historicism leads him in a very different direction from hermeneutical ontology, even though the starting-point may be the same.

A further implication of the second part of *Untimely Meditations* is the claim that 'unconsciousness' is an essential context for creativity and life. In this respect, a valuable by-product of the polemic against the irrationalism of late bourgeois philosophy carried out by many contemporary schools of thought, and by the 'orthodox' Marxism of

11

Lukács in particular, has been to call attention to the limited and ultimately contradictory character of purely vitalist and irrationalist interpretations of Nietzsche (and of all the early twentieth-century philosophical movements that refer more or less explicitly to him). Yet, on the other hand, if we look at other works by Lukács, such as the pre-Marxist *Soul and Form*, but also and above all *History and Class-Consciousness*, we find an astonishing fertility in the very themes that he himself later scorned as irrationalistic, in spite of his own indebtedness to them. The positivity of early twentieth-century 'irrationalism', even from a revolutionary viewpoint, is raised as a problem both by the early thought of Lukács and by the far more inspiring and coherent thought of Ernst Bloch. The fact that it is still unresolved suggests that the picture of Nietzsche as an irrationalist and a thinker of the era of bourgeois decadence requires thorough revision. Although this is a question that I cannot tackle here, echoes of it and of a possible alternative solution to it will none the less be found in what follows.[10]

In Nietzsche's discourse on the historical malady there is a third implication, one that is generally missed or at least relegated to a secondary position; and yet it may enable us to make considerable progress in our examination of the results and limitations of the hermeneutical overcoming of historicism. The historical malady is a malady, as we have seen, because an excess of historiographical awareness destroys the capacity to create new history. Nietzsche, as is suggested by the title of his essay, is interested in the 'usefulness[11] and disadvantages of history for life'. The term 'usefulness' is not being employed here in an ironic sense, as if Nietzsche were simply drawing a radical contrast between knowledge and action. He means it quite straightforwardly, for right at the beginning he states as the thesis of his essay that *'the unhistorical and the historical are necessary in equal measure for the health of an individual, of a people, and of a culture'*.[12] On the same page he describes the capacity to feel to a certain degree unhistorically as being more vital and fundamental . . . The unhistorical is like an atmosphere within which alone life can germinate . . . only by imposing limits on this unhistorical element by thinking, reflecting, comparing, distinguishing, drawing conclusions . . . only through the power of employing the past for the purposes of life and of again introducing into history that which has been done and is gone – did man become man: but with an excess of history man again ceases to exist.[13]

When Nietzsche envisages a kind of 'dialectic' between an enveloping unhistorical atmosphere and a historiographical awareness (itself inspired by the demand of 'life'), he is trying to put into words a concept of historical action that is not simply to be identified as a kind of blind acting which reflection cannot but follow, as though across a Hegelian gulf between the *in sich* and the *für sich*, between doing and knowing. The sort of creativity and historical productivity that Nietzsche wants to describe is rather an equilibrium between unconscious and conscious knowing, between a pure responding to the demands of life and an 'objective' reflection that 'thinks, rethinks, compares, distinguishes, puts together' – in other words, that fulfils the functions of 'reason'. Here the two aspects are not two separate moments; on one hand the activity of a reflection that compares and discerns is inspired and motivated by its usefulness for life, while on the other hand life itself, one may legitimately add, is not thought of in purely 'biological' terms, as persistently manifesting certain basic needs; for the man who feels as a necessity of life the need to reflect, to compare and to discern is a man who has been born into a particular culture, not into some 'nature' pure and simple. The delimitation of the correct and productive relationship between historiography and life is itself a historical and cultural fact. The development of Nietzsche's thought makes it increasingly clear that there is no such thing as 'life', with a characteristic essence on the basis of which we can measure with evolutionistic or some other criterion the validity and 'truth' of cultures or symbolic configurations.

If we bear all this in mind, we can also understand the significance of the use Nietzsche makes here of the concept of 'style', to which the equally important concept of 'horizon' is related. The delimitation of a given horizon cannot be described purely in terms of a contrast between a sphere of clarity and the obscurity that surrounds it. The concept of horizon[14] (which is frequently employed in contemporary hermeneutics, with reference to Nietzsche and phenomenology)[15] involves a much more complex relation between that which stands outside the horizon and that which lies within it. But what in fact matters most about the concept of horizon is the order of things articulated *within* it. It is to designate this delimitation of the horizon that Nietzsche utilizes the further concept of *style*, which ultimately underlies the whole second part of *Untimely Meditations*. The antithesis of the historical malady as the incapacity to produce history through an excess of historiographical awareness is not blind acting or the exaltation of the 'dark' powers of life but 'unity of artistic style', as a unity of all the manifestations of the life of a society and a people.[16] Style is the complete opposite of the '*remarkable antithesis*' that is typical of modern man: 'the remarkable antithesis between an interior which fails to correspond to any exterior and an exterior which fails to correspond to any interior'.[17] Here, the interior is historical knowing as the bare possession of 'contents' with respect to which man is a mere receptacle. But for Nietzsche the opposite of the historical malady is more generally stylistic unity as the unity between interior and exterior. This puts into a different perspective the 'vitalistic' contrast between a historiographical knowing which obstructs action and a way of acting that must by definition be unconscious.

None the less, the 'vitalistic' reading of Nietzsche's essay is not entirely illegitimate. In other words, it is true that he

14

views the separation of interior from exterior, historiography from action, and doing from knowing, as the fundamental feature of modern man's historical malady, and so himself remains a prisoner of this antithesis, with its unmistakably Hegelian roots. The passages I have been discussing from part two of *Untimely Meditations*, and particularly the ones in the first chapter on the 'dialectic' between unhistoricality (unconsciousness) and rational articulation, may also be read as putting forward a vision of history as a dialectic between 'life' and 'form' such that any definition of a horizon is possible both as an act of forgetting and at the same time as an act of interior rational articulation; every historical configuration amounts to forgetting inasmuch as it leaves outside its own sphere all 'the rest' of history and moreover forgets that it is itself surrounded by darkness. But the articulation of what is illuminated, in imposing itself as an exigency that is *universal*, and no longer merely intrinsic to a horizon, tends to dispel the darkness on which it lives, so that both creativity and the capacity to produce history become enfeebled and die. It is true that Nietzsche does not explicitly envisage a continual repetition of this antithesis, for the anti-historicism of the second part of *Untimely Meditations* also amounts to a refusal to theorize a general schema of history; and his struggle against decadence is inspired by a belief in the possibility of the restoration of a proper relationship between history and life, rather than by any belief in some inevitable alternation of creative periods with derivative and decadent ones. Yet even outside any such cyclical vision of history, it remains true that for the Nietzsche of the second part of *Untimely Meditations* there is ultimately a contrast that is still dialectical/Hegelian between awareness and forgetting, knowing and doing.

That the conclusion of the second part of *Untimely Meditations* not only may but must be read primarily in this sense is attested by its ultimate appeal to the 'eternalizing' powers of religion and art as remedies for the historical malady and more particularly for the domination of science. In the present cultural context at least, Nietzsche's essay sees the problem purely in terms of alternative supremacies: 'Is life to dominate knowledge and science, or is knowledge to dominate life? . . . There can be no doubt: life is the higher, the dominating force, for knowledge which annihilated life would have annihilated itself with it,' all this, at least 'up to the point at which [men] will be sufficiently healthy again to study history and, to the ends of life, to employ the past'.[18] But this possibility of a new epoch, with the recovery of a unity of style, remains ill-defined and uncertain; Nietzsche talks of life and knowledge in terms of conflict, and the eternalizing powers of art and religion do not here point towards a stylistic synthesis, but are essentially 'obscuring' forces, forces that are both suprahistorical and at the same time also unhistorical. In the conclusion to the ninth and penultimate chapter of the essay, the essence of creative historical action is seen in the capacity to act in an *unhistorical* way;[19] for the act by which man establishes the stable horizon within which there is a possibility of action is itself unhistorical.

It would be possible to give further evidence of the way that Nietzsche, in the second part of the *Untimely Meditations*, remains under the spell of Hegel. Even while he strives to conceive an ideal of historical existence capable of unifying interior with exterior, doing with knowing, a historical being that would be creative without at the same time being unreflective or vice-versa, his model remains 'Hegelian': it assumes that ultimately the motor of history is the gulf between doing and knowing, between *in sich* and *für sich*. The proof of this is his conclusion that the eternalizing forces – art and religion – offer the only escape from the deserts of historicist decadence.

It is art and religion that become two of the chief polemical targets in the initial section of *Human, all too Human*, the first work that really takes up where the second of the *Untimely*

Meditations leaves off, the one that initiates a new stage in Nietzsche's thought after the early works written under the spell of Schopenhauer and Wagner. The most superficial reading of *Human, all too Human* is enough to suggest that it cannot easily be reconciled with the antihistoricism of the second part of *Untimely Meditations*. However, rather than adopting a completely new viewpoint, Nietzsche seems now to be questing for a more authentic response to the demands manifested in the essay on history. None the less it is abundantly clear that both the polemic in *Human, all too Human* against art and religion and the return in that book to a broadly 'historicist'[20] position suggest the need for a cautious reappraisal of the conclusions drawn in the second part of *Untimely Meditations*. In particular we need to pay very careful attention to the problematic and contradictory aspects of these conclusions, which spur the further development of Nietzsche's thought.

All this has a particular relevance to the present discussion; for contemporary hermeneutical ontology, attacking historicism and presenting itself as an alternative to the historical malady, not only remains wedded to the conception of the historical malady expounded by Nietzsche in the second part of *Untimely Meditations*, but shows no sign of being aware of this or of overcoming the contradictions inherent in that conception. By contrast, when Nietzsche himself takes the problem a stage further, what results is a powerful tool for a critique of the limits of hermeneutical ontology.

What I refer to here as hermeneutical ontology is a philosophical movement that is ill-defined simply because it is so wide-ranging. The original impulse for this movement came from Heidegger, especially the later Heidegger, and it was reduced to a system in Hans-Georg Gadamer's *Truth and Method*, where the Heideggerian thematic is taken up and developed and the whole significance of its links with Dilthey and Husserl expounded in terms often suggestive of Hegel. It is Gadamer who detects and explores the affinities

17

to be found (underneath the undeniable differences) between the hermeneutical ontological conclusions of the late Heidegger on one hand and the later theory of Wittgenstein and the analytical schools that refer to this on the other.[21] The 'map' of hermeneutical ontology also extends over a wide sector of French culture (from Ricoeur to post-structuralists like Derrida, Foucault and Deleuze, and to some extent a thinker like Lacan too); it extends to a more limited and more uniform sector of Italian philosophy (Pareyson); and in addition it has ramifications of a theological and literary kind, as represented by the avant-garde of hermeneutics in present-day American culture (Robinson and Cobb, with their *New Frontiers in Theology*, and scholars like E. D. Hirsch or R. E. Palmer).[22] I am of course drawing up this highly problematical map from a hermeneutical, Heideggerian and Gadamerian viewpoint, and it is perfectly possible that neither the Anglo-Americans of the analytical school nor someone like Lacan, for example, would admit or would have admitted to belonging there. But I do believe that it has some plausibility, for there are present to some degree in all these styles of thinking certain crucial features of the hermeneutical perspective.

For the purposes of our discussion, hermeneutical ontology may be defined with reference to three elements, all of which relate to the fundamental notion of the hermeneutical circle. This is something that has persistently haunted reflection on the problem of interpretation, from the time of the earliest theories about the allegorical meaning of the Homeric poems to the typologism of patristic and mediaeval exegesis, to Luther's principle of *sola Scriptura*, and right up to Schleiermacher, Dilthey and Heidegger,[23] who was the first to give the idea a rigorous philosophical development, for he did not acknowledge it as a limit but as a positive possibility for knowledge, indeed as the only possibility available to Dasein for an experience of truth.[24] In its bare essentials the hermeneutical circle designates a particular reciprocal belonging between 'subject' and 'object' in interpretation, whereby these terms become necessarily invalidated, since they originated and developed within a perspective that assumed their separateness and antithesis and used them to give expression to these. Heidegger viewed interpretation as nothing other than the articulation of what is understood, and so always presupposing comprehension or precomprehension of the thing; for him this meant simply that knower and known belong to one another reciprocally prior to any explicit act of knowing and prior to any recognition of something as (*als*) something, so that the known is already within the horizon of the knower, but only because the knower is within the world that the known co-determines.

The three constitutive elements of what I call hermeneutical ontology (a Gadamerian term) can all be referred to this schematic formulation of the hermeneutical circle. The first of these elements is the rejection of 'objectivity' as an ideal of historical knowledge (and this means the rejection of the methodological model of the positive sciences). The second is the extension of the hermeneutical model to all knowledge, historical or otherwise, and the third is the linguistic nature of Being. Gadamer's way of putting this was to say that 'Being, which can be understood, is language.'[25] This sentence may be read either with two commas, one after *Being* and one after *understood*, or it may be read without any commas at all. But its true meaning is the one that would follow from the use of the commas, the one that affirms both the linguistic nature and the comprehensibility of all Being. Of course it is possible to think of a type of Being as incomprehensible, and such Being would not be language, but in that case the proposition would become a mere tautology. These three elements are also three successive stages in the construction of hermeneutical ontology, at least in the systematic form it has in *Truth and Method*. The first one indicates something that is particularly obvious in

19

Being and Time,[26] namely that hermeneutical ontology takes as its starting-point the problem of historical knowledge. Beginning from reflection on the inadequacy of the scientific/positive model with respect to historical knowledge and the human sciences, it moves on to a general critique of the positivistic model of scientific method. Hermeneutics lays claim to universality, a claim which is both concretized and founded in the theory of the linguistic nature of Being.

It is not part of my purpose here to give even a summary account of the stages in Gadamer's construction of this schema in *Truth and Method*. I shall merely note that the first stage is clearly a return to the Diltheyan inheritance, mediated through the Heidegger of *Being and Time* (see section 32 of that work, mentioned above). The second stage involves classifying every kind of knowledge as hermeneutical, implicitly including scientific knowledge, a move which subverts the positivistic cult of objectivity. This move is a direct consequence of the Heideggerian 'radicalization' of Dilthey; while Dilthey stopped short of explicitly theorizing the positive nature of the hermeneutical circle, Heidegger has no such inhibitions, and the ontological consequences of this for his thinking are momentous. For example, there is the central affirmation of the *Letter on Humanism*, where, in the thrown project that is Dasein, the 'thrower' is Being itself (LH p. 207). But the Diltheyan acknowledgement that historical knowledge cannot be understood and explained on the basis of the subject/object antithesis is not Heidegger's final word on the matter. On the contrary, two further problems inevitably emerge, namely, the question of how and why historiography ever came to accept this model as a valid one in the first place, and the broader question of whether and how far the subject/object model, with its relative canonization of objectivity, remains valid in general terms even if limited to the sphere of the so-called natural sciences. Reflection on these problems brings to light the fact that there is indeed no subject/object relation of the kind on which the positivistic model of knowledge is based.

This is the argument put forward by Heidegger in section 44 of *Being and Time*; there he states that what lies underneath every imaginable conformity of the proposition to the thing and all 'objective validity' of the knowledge of facts (which is of course the metaphysical conception of truth, recently and most coherently incarnated in the scientific/positive ideal of method) is a more primordial 'disclosedness'. He believes that it is this 'disclosedness' that initially makes possible any sort of conformity or unconformity; he holds that both the knower and the known belong primordially within it. Even scientific knowledge is interpretation insofar as it is an articulation of that which is understood. This articulation may still be guided, as is the case in modern science, by the general criterion of conformity, and by specific modes of verifying that;[27] but the establishment of these specific modes of articulation/interpretation is itself an 'event' that involves the most primordial disclosedness of Being, and the giving–concealing itself that constitutes its epochal nature. *Being and Time* shows 'tolerance' towards science and its criteria for verifying the conformity between proposition and thing, as does Heidegger's later work and that of Gadamer; but it is not at all clear whether or to what extent this 'tolerance' is to be taken at face value. In other words, it is not clear whether in fact Heidegger and his hermeneutical successors accord particular legitimacy to modern scientific methodology, as long as it remains within its specific limits. At all events, any such limits can certainly no longer be settled on the basis of the Diltheyan distinction between the natural and the human sciences, since acceptance of this would amount to a rejection of the universality of the interpretative structure of knowledge. But then, as is in fact the case with the development of Heideggerian thought, the proper limits of modern scientific methodology become 'limits' in a sense that is no longer purely descriptive but

21

evaluative – the limits of thought in the epoch of metaphysics, in the epoch of the forgetting of Being, the epoch of the reduction of the entity to an object. Modern science is not one of the possible forms of knowledge, i.e. one of the possible modes in which the internal articulation of a determinative precomprehension takes shape: for this would imply that such modes could be lined up next to one another on a transcendental level, as possible 'dimensions' of reason. Rather, it is an aspect of the epoch of Being in which we find ourselves, an epoch which is also that of historicism in its various forms, historicism as both a general philosophy of history and a scientific model of historiography.

The classification of all knowledge as hermeneutical further involves the reaffirmation, though in a novel way, of the notion of the historicity of knowledge: it means that historiographical knowledge and every other type of knowing are never merely 'contemplation' of objects, but rather action that modifies the context to which it belongs and of which it becomes a part. In developing his ontological thinking Heidegger tends to think this historicity radically through in terms of the epochality of Being; for him our knowing is now completely saturated with the metaphysical forgetting of Being and this forgetting is *defined* by Being itself, so that it cannot be altered by a mere change of attitude on man's part. But Heidegger's 'hermeneutical' followers generally tend to pick up only the blander and less provocative aspects of this discourse. For them, the universality of hermeneutics and the historicity of knowledge signify merely that history grows as a perpetual interpretative process. To know is to interpret, but to interpret is also to produce new history. In this 'eirenic' perspective, all the dramatic force in the Heideggerian idea of metaphysics is lost. *Truth and Method*, for example, betrays little sign of Heidegger's dramatic vision of the history of western civilization. This modification and attenuation that Heideggerian thinking on the epochal nature of Being and on metaphysics undergoes at the hands of his hermeneutical successors has significant consequences for the problem with which I am concerned, and I shall have occasion to return to it.

The third of the characteristic theses of hermeneutical ontology is also directly linked to the general idea of the hermeneutical circle, and at the same time it represents a coherent conclusion to the two preceding theses. The centrality of language in the development of the ontological problem is already a feature in *Being and Time*, where there is a whole play of relations established between Being-in-the-world and meaningfulness, although it is not fully worked out until the writings that follow. Gadamer takes on board this more developed Heideggerian treatment, but at the same time he somehow manages to render it too schematic and oversimplified; he makes it an implicit corollary of the other two theses. In his view, the hermeneutical nature of experience is most evident when we reflect on the problem of historical knowledge, where it seems obvious that the subject-object model is no longer applicable; but then in addition, when we reflect on how and why the methodological model of the positive sciences has emerged and then imposed itself on the human sciences, it becomes clear that every type of knowledge and experience of the truth is in fact hermeneutical. However, this universalization of the hermeneutic implies that all experience and all knowledge is to be understood as linguistic. As I have already said, in Gadamer there is no explicit attempt to apply hermeneutics systematically to science, in the sense of the science of nature. But neither can it be said that the Diltheyan dichotomy is still a valid one for him. He does not see the hermeneutical character of experience as depending solely on the fact that between linguistic experience and the other modes of experience an 'analogy' (in scholastic terms, an analogy of proportionality) may be drawn: in that we are 'called' by the various 'realities' of experience *just as* we are called by the messages transmitted by language. It depends much more essentially on the fact that all experience of the world is *mediated* through language, and therefore is primarily a linguistic event, discourse or dialogue of question and answer. This means that there is an analogy 'of attribution' between experience in general and linguistic experience.[28] The principle that sums up Gadamer's hermeneutical ontology – 'Being, which can be understood, is language' – thus suggests by its double implication a vision of history as a transmission of messages or a dialogue of question and answer, where language is the fundamental mode in which Being occurs. We already belong to that which is transmitted to us, we are *angesprochen* by the call that tradition addresses to us, but not because we already belong to the 'world' as expressed in linguistic experience before and beyond that linguistic experience; Being is not something more vast than language and prior to it. Rather, the preliminary belonging to Being is a preliminary and primordial belonging to language; Being is history, and history of language.

There is an initial consequence of this vision of Being and history as a transmission of calls, as a dialectic/dialogic of question and answer, in which the respondent is always already constituted by the fact of being called. It is that the interpretation of history, and indeed knowledge in general, is not a process of decipherment or a going back from the sign to the signified understood as the extralinguistic object to which the word 'refers'. The interpretation of history is rather a dialogue in which the real *Sache*, the real question at issue, is that 'fusion of horizons' discussed by Gadamer,[29] a fusion in which the 'world' with its 'objects' is continually reconstructed and in some sense 'grows' in being by the process of interpretation.[30] There are two implications here: first, the model of the objectivity of historical awareness is replaced by the model of the historiographical act as dialogical, i.e. as a (new) historical event. When Gadamer talks about *Wirkungsgeschichte* and *wirkungsgeschichtliches Bewusstsein*, he is ultimately referring to the fact that the *objective*

24

truth of the past historical event cannot be other than what the event has been and is from the moment of its first having happened until today; this includes its addressing a call to us and the dialogue that it initiates with us and we with it.[31] Second, interpretation is an *in(de)finite* process in which every response changes and modifies the character of the call to the extent that it affects the very being of that which calls as the 'other' in the dialogue; far from closing the discourse, it actually stimulates further questions. The definitiveness (or at least the tendency towards definitiveness) of the 'decipherment' – i.e. the completion of the process of going back from the sign to the signified, with the consequent relegation of the sign to inessentiality – is replaced by the autonomous life of language, lived in dialogue. This also constitutes a rejection of the Hegelian solution, which substituted for the relation of decipherment the phenomenological itinerary in which the truth of the particular event was manifested only in the totality of the process when completed. For here there seems to persist the implication of an 'objectivist' model of ultimate self-transparency, and in the end this seemed to mean the same model of decipherment, albeit enlarged to include the historical becoming of interpretations, but still always within a horizon dominated by the 'monological' essence of modern rationalism.[32] A vision of history as the history of language and as open dialogue is therefore coessential to hermeneutical ontology. On the basis of premises similar to Gadamer's, Luigi Pareyson explicitly names this the infinity of interpretation.[33]

To what extent does hermeneutical ontology as I have outlined it truly succeed in overcoming the 'historical malady' as described and attacked by Nietzsche? This first raises the question of whether the historical malady should in fact primarily be identified with historiography inspired by methodological models of 'scientific' objectivity, for this might also seem to involve an exclusion, or at least a neglect, of that aspect of historiography itself which is authentically historical (i.e. active, productive and innovative). If such an identification be correct, then hermeneutical ontology clearly represents a way of pushing to an extreme and thereby resolving the demands raised in the second part of *Untimely Meditations*. However, Nietzsche stigmatized historiographical objectivism as a malady insofar as it was the expression of a dichotomy between interior and exterior, between doing and knowing. He saw the excessive historiographical awareness of the nineteenth century (which has developed even further in our own time) as opposed to the needs of life because it implied an inability to 'digest' cognitive material, so that it was impossible to act on the basis of such knowledge with coherence of style. But this second and more radical aspect of the problem of the historical malady does not seem to receive sufficient attention in hermeneutical ontology. For Nietzsche, historiographical objectivism was only a facet of the theory/practice dichotomy; it had to be opposed because it was based on the assumption that to become aware of an ever-growing number of facts about the past was a value in itself, independently of any reference to present or future problems. For hermeneutics, on the other hand, historiographical objectivism is above all an error in methodology and it does not relate to the theory/practice dichotomy so much as to the illegitimate domination of the field of the human sciences by the methodology of the positive sciences. It is evident that, through Heidegger's thinking on metaphysics and its crucial significance in determining the historical existence of western (and latterly of technological) man, we can see that the methodological error of taking scientific objectivity as a universal model is basically bound up with the theory/practice dichotomy, something peculiar to the metaphysical mentality. But hermeneutical ontology does not bring out this mediation. Therefore there is a very real danger that the affirmation of the hermeneutical and linguistic essence of every historical happening may become equivalent to a legitimation of all theoretical activity insofar as it is always already *de facto* practice.[34] And this must surely be connected with a fact whose apparent strangeness quickly vanishes on further consideration, the fact that hermeneutical onto-logy fails to offer – whether because it cannot or will not – methodological guidelines for the actual concrete task of interpretation. It supposes that every act of knowledge is already of its essence hermeneutical and cannot be 'objective' in the sense appropriate to the scientific method. Thus Gadamer has no wish to teach us anything that we cannot and do not in fact already do: he is content to make explicit what happens in every kind of knowing, starting with historiographical knowing, and ending with a redefinition of experience *in terms of what it already actually is.*

This way of proceeding, involving as it does the uncov-ering of the 'true' and 'already given' structure of historical knowledge and then of all experience and indeed of existence itself, understood as existing in the Being that is language, looks all too much like a new metaphysical 'theory'; as such it certainly cannot answer the requirements laid down by Nietzsche, and still less the spirit of Heidegger's thought, to which it refers more explicitly.

In Heidegger, both the discovery of the hermeneutical circle in *Being and Time* and the subsequent gradual elucida-tion of the particular nexus of Being and language always go along with an acute awareness of the problematic nature of these so-called 'structures'. While in *Being and Time* interpre-tation is the internal articulation of a precomprehension that constitutes *Dasein*, the latter none the less has in common with all existentials that it is involved in the more general alternatives of authentic or inauthentic existence (cf. BT pp. 40, 44). This needs to be borne in mind if we are to understand why even in this vision of knowledge as the internal articulation of an always already available pre-comprehension, there is still the need for a 'violent' act of discovery of the truth, such as the one called for by the phenomenological method as Heidegger outlines it in the introduction to *Being and Time*. In his subsequent works the affirmation of the Being-language nexus is always linked with the problem of metaphysics as a historical presentation of Being, a presentation that involves an unconcealing/concealing: this unconcealing/concealing belongs above all to Being, and yet in spite or perhaps because of this belonging to Being, it fundamentally concerns our historicity, determining its 'fallen' condition in the metaphysical world of *Seinsvergessenheit*. This is one of two reasons why Heidegger never manages to say, as Gadamer does in his formula mentioned above, that *Being is language*. (The other reason is related to this one; it is the impossibility of saying that Being *is* this or that, or indeed of using the verb 'to be' as a copula at all.)

For Heidegger, the Being-language nexus, the linguistic and therefore also hermeneutical character of human experience of the world, are both deeply problematic. Indeed, it could be said that they are *the* problem that constitutes our existence in the epoch of accomplished metaphysics. In Gadamer and hermeneutical ontology all this becomes a description of Being, a theory of the structure of the human condition, of the finitude of existence.

It is in this light that we should look at Habermas's critique of Gadamer.[35] Habermas argues that hermeneutics as a philosophical discipline, or indeed *tout court* as *the* philosophical discipline *par excellence*, presupposes a break in tradition. (And it is true that both ancient and modern hermeneutics originated and developed at moments when there was an exceptionally strong sense of the need to restore a threatened, interrupted, or at the very least uncertain continuity: patristics was concerned with the continuity between the Old and New Testaments, as were classical studies of more modern times with the continuity between Humanism and their day.) At the same time, Habermas accuses hermeneutics of evading the problem posed by such breaks; for in affirming that everything in history consists in the transmission of messages, in dialectic/dialogic of questions and answers, Gadamer describes Being/language (the linguistic nature of experience) *as if* tradition were really a *continuum*. The statement 'Being, which can be understood, is language' means that Being is language, and consequently that language is not as such first and foremost a pure instrument of communication, a sign to be deciphered by going back exhaustively to an extra-linguistic object; it is an event of Being itself. So why is it that the western tradition has ultimately transmitted to us a conception of language as sign, to be assessed by its actual capacity for 'objective' reference, and offering itself to the essential experience of decipherment, with all those implications that in Heidegger attach to metaphysics and the forgetting of Being? Hermeneutical ontology simply fails to discuss this whole problem; it remains in this fundamental and crucial sense devoid of 'methodological' guidelines; not for the human sciences, but for existence, which needs such guidelines if it is to establish itself *de facto* in the linguisticality that is attributed *de jure* to Being. Heidegger is well aware of the fact that in late metaphysical society (and we could equally well call it late capitalist society) language is far from prevailing (*'wesen'*) in its pure essence as the event of Being. Not only has man 'misunderstood' language, taking it as essentially sign; language actually *prevails* as such, while the world of objects likewise *prevails* as independent, and is there purely to be accepted and described in accordance with criteria of rigorous objectivity. However Heidegger may interpret and theorize it, the domination of objectivity remains a fact of domination, and it cannot as such be overcome merely through the theoretical recognition of a methodological error.

If it is true that the historical malady is basically characterized by a split between theory and practice, involving a lack of adequation between doing and knowing, while historical action is condemned either to be unconscious or not to be action, then hermeneutical ontology fails authentically to overcome the problem, precisely to the extent that it forgets this problem of the unity of theory and practice *as a problem*. If my hypothesis about the conclusions drawn in the second part of *Untimely Meditations* is correct, they offered no finality for Nietzsche; in the ensuing works, from *Human, all too Human* onwards, it dawned on him with ever-increasing clarity that the ways out he had originally proposed – the eternalizing forces of art and religion – were still vitiated by the very separation of doing from knowing that constituted the malady as malady.

Hermeneutical ontology evades the problem of the unification of doing and knowing. It considers this problem resolved by a theoretical recognition of the linguistic and hermeneutical character of existence, but all the while it remains committed to the separation of theory from practice. This separation is not discussed in hermeneutical ontology; it is pushed back and repressed as it were – but it surfaces again, just like things that are repressed in psychoanalytical theory or, in the theory of interpretation itself, 'prejudices' that are not recognized or not accepted as such. The separation makes its presence felt both in the results of this type of thinking and in its prevailing *Stimmung*. It views the infinity of the interpretative process as ultimately only a correlative of the finitude of man. Gadamer's notion of experience reflects the fundamental features of Hegelian *Erfahrung*, 'having experiences' – in other words, changing, running up against the unexpected and the negative, and hence for Gadamer also being experienced or 'having lived', being aware of the relativity and ephemerality of the human: this is essentially in harmony with a Goethian/Diltheyan form of wisdom, in which history again figures as essentially the passing of things.[36]

Lived in this way, the infinity of interpretation, and the perpetual repetition of the dialectic/dialogic of question and answer as the very marrow of history, has the feel of wandering or exile. And the term 'wandering' is of course often favoured by Heidegger as a way of describing the condition of thought *in the epoch of metaphysics*: but in fact it does not at all define the essence of man. From this point of view, the stress in hermeneutics on the finitude of man and the infinity of interpretation (of history) still looks like a moment within the epoch of metaphysics, which can therefore hardly claim to be overcoming metaphysics. Finitude, wandering and exile, or even simply the infinity of the interpretative process, are all expressions that involve the persistence of the separation of theory from practice, never overcome because never discussed.

It is true that the Heideggerian idea of ontological difference may be read as involving a discussion of this dichotomy. Significantly, however, it is an idea that cannot be found in *Truth and Method*, nor indeed is it to be found in hermeneutical ontology in general. Heidegger discusses difference, and man's condition of separation and exile from Being thereby also becomes a problem by implication, though to what extent is debatable. The issue is however ignored by his hermeneutical followers, for whom difference is felt as something repressed that resurfaces. In their thought, the authenticity/inauthenticity thematic, together with its development in the problem of overcoming metaphysics, is retransformed into a 'metaphysical' acceptance of the finitude of Dasein as the infinity of the interpretative process.

To put it another way, the problem that hermeneutical ontology leaves undiscussed is this one: if there is an infinity of interpretation, and if we conceive this, as hermeneutical ontology does, in a way that is substantially inseparable from the finitude of existence, does this not also necessarily imply a permanent split between existence and meaning, between doing and knowing? This in turn would mean that ultimately the infinity of interpretation is nothing but the old

Hegelian gulf between *in sich* and *für sich* as the motor for the whole phenomenological process and for the whole history of the spirit. Hermeneutics objects that the complete identification of doing with knowing and of existence with meaning would be equivalent to nothing less than the end of history in the perfect self-transparency of the absolute Hegelian spirit; and in making this objection, incidentally, hermeneutics is much closer to Kierkegaardian existentialism than to Heidegger. But the objection still seems to take Hegel's terminology for granted: it seems to imply that historical action is either at least partly unconscious or else not action at all but pure retrospective contemplation, as Nietzsche supposed in the second part of *Untimely Meditations*. To Gadamer the unity of doing and knowing seems possible only in the monological form of the Hegelian system. The alleged overcoming of the historical malady (or historical consciousness) thus becomes yet another canonization of history as pure passing, at least in the strict sense in which all that is inessential is passing (which is of course what all existence is when separated from its meaning). We are back once more with the paralysing wisdom of the disciple of Heraclitus. This way of looking at things is much less indebted to Heidegger and Nietzsche than it is to Dilthey and the comprehensively 'retrospective' character of his vision of history.

All of this, conspicuously absent from the conclusions drawn by hermeneutical ontology, puts a question mark against its claim to represent an overcoming of historical consciousness. The briefest of glances at the way Nietzsche's thought evolves after *Human, all too Human*, shows that any such overcoming will require us to tackle (at both the theoretical and the practical level) the dichotomy that dominates western man; a dichotomy that underlies all the recurrent philosophical appeals to the 'finitude' of existence in the face of the 'totalizing claims' of dialectical thought. To put it crudely, as we have to do here, it must be said that the Nietzschean idea of the *Uebermensch* can only be understood and explained if it is seen as a more than theoretical effort to construct a type of man capable of living the unity of existence and meaning, of doing and knowing, *historically* (and therefore still in time, in becoming, not in the motion-less self-transparency of the Hegelian absolute spirit). There is a possibility of going beyond the historical malady and historical 'consciousness' solely *in so far as one establishes the possibility of a history that is not malady*, a history that does not have as its motor the gulf between *in sich* and *für sich*. Both in its theoretical content and in the theoretical/practical dimen-sion it has, and of which Nietzsche is well aware, this problem constitutes the focus of all Nietzsche's work after his abandonment of his youthful veneration for Schopen-hauer and Wagner. The questions left unresolved in the second part of *Untimely Meditations* are thus the inspiration for the development of this thought, which may with justification be read entirely in the light of the question of historicism.

Simply as an indication of the meaning I have attributed to this Nietzschean enterprise, it is worth pondering at this point a suggestive passage in Sartre's *The Problem of Method*, (which in the original appears as the introduction to the *Critique de la Raison dialectique*). For this reads as an explicit 'challenge' to 'hermeneutical reason' and its affirmation of the infinity of the interpretative process, even if Sartre himself did not intend it primarily as such.

> Marxism in the nineteenth century is a gigantic attempt not only to make History but to get a grip on it, practically and theoretically . . . Thus the plurality of *the meanings* of History can be discovered and posited for itself only upon the ground of a future totalization . . . Our historical task, at the heart of this polyvalent world, is to bring closer the moment

when History will have *only one meaning*, when it will tend to be dissolved in the concrete men who will make it in common.[37]

This reference to Sartre is to be taken not as a conclusion but as a signpost. His argument makes it seem even more obvious that the conclusions of hermeneutical ontology are bound up with that vision of history as pure happening which retains something of a hold on Nietzsche in the second part of *Untimely Meditations*. This is why, from the perspective of hermeneutical ontology, every claim to totality simply looks like the danger of an end to history, the risk of the absolutization of monologue in its Hegelian form. Paradoxically, it is in a characteristically and peculiarly Hegelian sense that hermeneutical ontology can conceive of history in action solely as *malady*, that is as a gulf between Being and meaning, between doing and knowing, between theory and practice. But the fact is that the malady cannot be overcome unless the foundation is laid for a history that is not malady, not separation between interior and exterior, not absence of style. Hermeneutical ontology is quite right to view history as the history of language, the pure transmission of messages, or, to use terms closer to those of Nietzsche, as the freedom of the world of symbols. The word is not first and foremost the sign of a world independent of language; history is the history of words, it is dialogue, much more primordially and fundamentally than it is the history of 'things'. But what is hard to understand in these propositions is the true bearing of the 'is': in hermeneutical ontology, despite all its references to Heidegger, this 'is' is still always the 'is' of metaphysics and hence descriptive of essences that are present at hand. By contrast, Nietzsche, Heidegger, and more recently Sartre, have each in his own way grasped the problematic nature of this 'is'. The liberation of the world of symbols from its subjection to a prevailing 'reality' that is prior to it, that dominates it and is the measure of it through

criteria such as that of objectivity – this liberation is ultimately what is represented by the affirmation of the linguistic nature of Being. And it is an act that requires a
theoretical/practical movement involving something more
complex than simply becoming aware of the notion of the
hermeneutical circle and its implications. For Heidegger
what is required is the 'step back' from metaphysical/
representative thought to the thought of Being as recollection, *Andenken*. For Nietzsche it is the construction of the
superman, while for Sartre it is the founding of a new way of
living out intersubjectivity, leading to the final conquest of
the inertia of that counterfinality which prevails in a world of
penury and struggle.

Over against hermeneutical 'wisdom' as the acceptance of
finitude there stands experience as affirmed by Nietzsche, the
effort to construct a new subject capable of living the unity
of being and meaning, doing and knowing; or, in other
words, capable of experiencing Hegel's absolute knowledge
historically (without ending in immobility); in other words,
capable of living in the freedom of the symbolic.

Is it possible for there to be a historical action bearing
along with it from the beginning its own meaning, and not
liable to fall back into the inertia of counterfinality? Is there a
possible interpretation that means a way of living out
symbols, an interpretation that is dance and play as with
Zarathustra, and not a persistent re-emergence of the transcendence of meaning, a wandering, an exercise in finitude?
Can there be a production of symbols that is not based on the
repression/sublimation structure? Can there in this sense be
an overcoming of metaphysics?

This is the conclusion, or rather the new starting-point, to
which we are led in reflecting on the limitations of hermeneutical ontology from the point of view of the historical
malady. The totalization to which these questions point us is
always still in the future: yet perhaps nothing else but this
can confer on the periods of history a character that is

different from that of pure passing (the passing of the inessential, separated from its meaning) which is what constitutes it as malady.

Notes

1   *Truth and Method*, London, 1975 and 1979. The second part of this work is particularly concerned with the critique of historical consciousness.
2   See e.g. *Truth and Method*, pp. 271ff.
3   Heidegger's thought, too, is bound up not simply with the Nietzschean problematic in general, but also specifically with the idea of a historical malady. I am thinking for instance of the essay 'The Age of the World Picture' (in Martin Heidegger, *The Question concerning Technology and other Essays*, translated and edited by William Lovitt, New York and Toronto, 1977, pp. 115–54), and also in general of Heidegger's writings on Nietzsche, where the theme of historicism is all-pervasive.
4   See below my outline of a 'map' of the hermeneutical thematic in contemporary thought.
5   J.-P. Sartre, *Critique of Dialectical Reason*, trans. Alan Sheridan Smith, vol. 1, *Theory of Practical Ensembles*, London, 1976. For further discussion of this topic, as well as for additional bibliographical material, see my 'L'esistenzialismo di J.-P. Sartre', in *Terzo programma*, 1972, fasc. 2.
6   *Untimely Meditations*, Part II, 'On the uses and disadvantages of history for life' (1874), trans. R. J. Hollingdale, Cambridge, 1983. From now on I shall refer to this as UM II, followed by the chapter and page numbers as appropriate. On the 'historical malady' see UM II pp. 120ff.
7   I have undertaken a more lengthy and detailed analysis of this essay by Nietzsche in my article 'Nichilismo e problema del tempo in Nietzsche' in *Pascal e Nietzsche, Quaderni dell'Archivio di Filosofia*, 1962. The reader is referred to this for discussion of the actual content of Nietzsche's text, which is

only briefly alluded to here. The approach adopted in that study is very different from the one I pursue here, a fact which I believe to be of more than merely biographical interest. Given that everything that 'one' writes is the sign of a particular cultural moment, there is a value in setting the two approaches against each other: they indicate the change in perspective that has recently taken place with respect to the theme of the malady of history and historicism etc. . . (1974).

8   UM II pp. 62–3.
9   UM II p. 77.
10 For further discussion of this see my *Il soggetto e la maschera. Nietzsche e il problema della liberazione*, 2nd ed., Milan, 1979.
11 In the English translation referred to in the present volume, R. J. Hollingdale renders the word as 'use', but to render it as 'usefulness' fits in better with Vattimo's argument here. (Translator's note.)
12 UM II p. 63; the italics are Nietzsche's.
13 Ibid.
14 UM II pp. 115, 120.
15 Cf. *Truth and Method*, pp. 269ff.
16 UM II p. 79.
17 UM II p. 78.
18 UM II pp. 121, 122.
19 UM II p. 115.
20 The first volume of *Human, all too Human* begins with an aphorism that sets out a programme for a 'historical' type of philosophizing. Note also aphorism 292, where the significance of this return to history on Nietzsche's part is expounded in a highly suggestive manner, with hints of a kind of Nietzschean 'phenomenology of the spirit'. On this whole question, see the second section of my *Il soggetto e la maschera*.
21 Gadamer refers explicitly to Wittgenstein in relation to the concept of play and language, in a note in the foreword to *Truth and Method* (p. xxiv, n.12). But nowadays there are a huge number of studies, especially in Germany, that purport to establish connections between hermeneutical ontology and the later Wittgenstein; I am thinking particularly of the work of K. O. Apel. See also G. Radnitzky, *Contemporary Schools of Metascience*, vol. 2, Göteborg, 1970.

22 R. Palmer, *Hermeneutics*, Evanston, Ill., 1969; E. D. Hirsch, *Validity and Interpretation*, New Haven, 1967.

23 In this connection see the article 'Hermeneutik' by G. Ebeling in the encyclopedia, *Die Religion in Geschichte und Gegenwart*, and the introduction to my *Schleiermacher filosofo dell'interpretazione*, Milan, 1967.

24 BT p. 28.

25 *Truth and Method*, p. 432.

26 The problem that provides the starting-point for *Being and Time*, the problem of the meaning of Being, is determined, as much as and indeed more than by the phenomenological problematic of regional ontologies and fundamental ontology, by the question of how freedom can be thought, and therefore how history can be thought, within the categories of metaphysics. O. Pöggeler, in *Martin Heidegger's Path of Thinking*, trans. D. Magarshak and S. Barber, Atlantic Highlands, 1987, has highlighted the importance of the religious problem, and more specifically the problem of the encounter between the new contents of the Christian message and the metaphysical schemas of Greek philosophy, during the preparation of *Being and Time* in the Freiburg years. But in actual fact the question of how it is possible to think the contents of Christian theology in the language of metaphysics is at bottom the same as the question of whether the categories of Greek metaphysics are adequate to describe historical existence.

27 Cf. BT p. 262: 'In proposing our "definition" of "truth" we have not *shaken off* the tradition, but we have *appropriated* it primordially': it is at least *possible* to read this in a sense favourable to my argument.

28 This may throw light on the way that in contemporary culture linguistics, and especially Saussurean linguistics, has increasingly taken on the role of a model for the human sciences; it raises the question whether this model could and should perhaps be extended in general to all the sciences.

29 *Truth and Method*, pp. 273–4, 337 and *passim*.

30 See for example those pages in *Truth and Method* that deal with the ontological significance of the image, and in which

Gadamer talks explicitly about the 'increase of being' produced by the image on the model (p. 134). There is a principle here that can easily be extended to the manner in which Gadamer conceives of history and interpretation.

31 On *Wirkungsgeschichte* and related themes see *Truth and Method*, pp. 267ff. and *passim*.

32 Cf. *Truth and Method*, pp. 346–7.

33 Cf. *Estetica, Teoria della formatività*, 2nd ed., Bologna, 1960, and *Verità e interpretazione*, Milan, 1971.

34 In the same way, with their idea of 'theoretical practice', Althusser and his followers understand the division of labour non-dialectically and therefore provide a justification for intellectual work as it is in the world of late capitalism. Much of present-day French philosophy and criticism is given up to the old exercises in rhetoric, gaily pursued as the true path of revolution.

35 Cf. J. Habermas, *On the Logic of the Social Sciences*, trans. S. W. Nicholson and J. A. Stark, Cambridge, 1988.

36 See, for example, *Truth and Method*, p. 325.

37 J.-P. Sartre, *The Problem of Method*, trans. H. E. Barnes, London, 1964, pp. 89–90.

2

The Decline of the Subject and the Problem of Testimony

AN Y appeal to the idea of testimony nowadays can justifiably be labelled anachronistic. At least for anyone who was educated during the early postwar period in Europe, the word 'testimony' seems inextricably linked to a well-defined era in the history of European culture, namely, the era of existentialism. Testimony, as a philosophical and theological term, is a reminder of the profound intensity with which from the time of Kierkegaard existentialism has always viewed the unrepeatable existence of the individual and his particular and highly personal relationship with truth, a relationship to which a person commits himself wholly, exclusively and in isolation. There is a clear instance of this in Jaspers' celebrated thesis on Galileo and Bruno, according to which Galileo's retraction in the face of the Inquisition does nothing to impugn the scientifically demonstrable truth of the heliocentric theory, whereas Bruno's philosophical truth subsists only in the 'testimony' he bears to it. Thus Bruno could not retract without at the same time destroying the truth of his philosophy.[1] Hence a scientific truth is ahistorical and universal, while philosophical truth has no other meaning than to be the truth of the existence of the one who professes it and propounds it to the world.

Today's philosophical climate shows little interest in this kind of subject and is in general unreceptive to the themes of

40

'classic' existentialism, such as the individual, freedom to choose, responsibility, death and *Angst*: indifference to such themes is indeed peculiarly characteristic of those who claim none the less to be heirs to existentialism. Such is the case with French structuralism, for example, which unquestionably picks up Heideggerian themes, even if on occasion only to travesty them. And on a very different level of theoretical profundity there is Gadamer's hermeneutical ontology, a theory of interpretation in which it is difficult to single out any determinate function corresponding to the 'person'. Of late there has in fact been a wave of 'impersonalism' both at the level of the most penetrating philosophical research and at the level of more fleeting cultural trends. Although this is not the place to examine the phenomenon in depth, I certainly do not believe that it has only a negative influence and ought to be resisted, rather, it is a symptom of a real turn in our way of thinking and a transformation in the fundamental conditions of existence. Any discourse on testimony must begin from a recognition and analysis of this fact, which is connected with the decline of existentialism and at a deeper level with the crisis of the notion of the subject itself.

To recognize the reasons for speaking of the 'anachronistic' flavour of a concept like that of testimony, we might consider the work of the two authors from whom, perhaps more than anyone else, the current 'impersonalistic' trend in philosophy and culture takes its rise, namely Nietzsche and Heidegger. They are the ones above all whose assumptions have made an idea like that of testimony seem out of date, that is, through their initiation of a radical critique of the notion of the subject, the subject as constituted and consolidated from Descartes onwards on the basis of a tradition identifiable with that of classicism and Christianity. In a nutshell, the expression 'bourgeois/Christian subject' captures the constitutive features of this subject, and is not unfaithful to the deeper intentions of Nietzsche and Heidegger.

41

Nietzsche often expresses himself trenchantly and significantly on testimony in its most extreme and emblematic form as martyrdom. The theme emerges in *Zarathustra* part II (' of the priests') where the 'probative' value of Christian martyrdom is completely discredited. He dismisses as utterly absurd the idea that a truth may be demonstrated by the shedding of blood. Indeed, 'blood is the worst witness of truth; blood poisons and transforms the purest teaching into delusion and hatred of the heart.' Nor is this all: he writes in *The AntiChrist*: 'martyrs have *harmed* truth', for the foolish and the naive are taken in by martyrdom; they are always too ready to suppose that a cause for the sake of which someone faces death cannot be without value.[2]

The important thing here for my purposes, as indeed for Nietzsche himself, is not so much the distinction between the *quaestio iuris* of the truth-value of a proposition and the *quaestio facti* of the subjective evidence on the basis of which a person sacrifices his life in wishing to affirm that proposition. Aside from anything else, traditional Christian thinking about martyrdom has never gone so far as to maintain that it amounts to a true and proper 'proof' of the truth of Christianity. Nor does Nietzsche for his part hold that there is a purely logico-metaphysical *quaestio iuris* regarding truth-value that can be set against the simple fact of the irresistible subjective evidence on the basis of which a person is willing to die for a cause. Rather, for Nietzsche everything is reducible to a *quaestio facti*: and this is the meaning of the critique of the idea of evidence that he initiates in the essay 'On Truth and Falsity in their Ultramoral Sense' and continues right up to the notes for *The Will to Power*. In the latter he goes as far as to state baldly that my inability to conceive the contrary of a given proposition as possible is very far from demonstrating the truth of it. In fact it proves that the proposition is false, for it is thereby revealed to be merely a determinative condition for the preservation and development of a certain type of life, namely my own and the life of my world. My accepting it for true is thus completely the opposite of the detached and objective view of the scientist: it is an act that is supremely passionate and committed and therefore supremely open to error, at least according to the traditional criteria for objectivity.[3] Here again though, Nietzsche's concern is not to contrast a possibly objective and detached way of knowing the truth with a partisan distortion of it; in his eyes evidence is itself tainted with this basic 'vice'. What seems obvious and clear to me, even when the evidence for it is obtained by way of a highly stringent discipline such as that of the 'scientific method', seems so only within a framework of needs that belong to a 'particular form of life', as Nietzsche often underlines, especially in *The Will to Power*.

This is the meaning of Nietzsche's reduction of truth to morality. Whenever a proposition seems evident, there operates a series of historical premises and predispositions towards acceptance or rejection on the part of the subject, and these predispositions are guided by an overriding interest in the preservation and development not simply of 'life' as such, but of a particular form of life. This is not, however, the same as the mere reduction of a prioris, or of ordering schemas of experience, to historical structures, to biological, psychological or social heredity, as in a certain type of evolutionistic positivism. Or at least we could say this: Nietzsche's affirmation of the historicity of the a priori, as we might call it, is a great deal more radical than it is in positivism. There are two reasons for this: on one hand, he is entirely free from evolutionistic prejudice, so that for him the historicity of the a priori also implies its non-necessity and relative fortuitousness. Our mode of being in the world and our criteria for distinguishing true from false are not those that are dictated by 'life' as such, they are not the only or the best ones for *life in general*. They are those appropriate to a particular form of life, constituted and consolidated as a precise and particular configuration of relations of domination, relations that could have been and may be other than they are. In fact the doctrine of the superman amounts to a polemic against evolutionism; it maintains that modern man, far from being the culmination of a process of evolution, is in reality a form that must be changed and overcome, not by further development but by nothing less than a mutation.

A second feature of this Nietzschean 'historicity of the a priori' entails its development into a theory of the stratified structure of consciousness. And this brings us to the real root of Nietzsche's rejection of martyrdom and testimony. As we have seen, Nietzsche rejects the value of martyrdom on the grounds that irresistible evidence is no sign of truth, since it merely attests to the conformity between a given proposition and the interests of a certain form of life to which the individual belongs. His real point, however, is not simply that evidence itself is only a sign of such conformity, but that even the criterion of evidence as the benchmark of truth is a constitutive aspect of a certain historical form of life, the one to which we belong. When evidence (in Cartesian terms, a clear and distinct idea) is taken as the hallmark and distinctive criterion of truth, this is a cultural phenomenon that is constitutive of a civilization in which man is conceived and defined in terms of consciousness and the hegemony of conscious knowing over every other aspect of the personality.

To put it crudely, the martyr thinks that truth is something he has at his disposal,[4] yet in reality what he thinks of as true is only that which conforms to certain practical/ utilitarian schemas that he shares with his particular epoch, with his historical 'species'. And this basic affirmation quickly opens the way to a further step. When I assert that something is true inasmuch as it is evident, what goes on in me is actually quite different from what seems to me to be going on. While my consciousness talks about what is true and what is false, believing itself to be detached and objective in a scientific way, in reality it is doing nothing else but cultivating and favouring the assertion of its own interests and those of the group or epoch or social class to which it belongs and which it unconsciously represents. Thus there is more going on in the act of knowing than is apparent to consciousness; on the contrary, what it does is to reflect within itself a process that has already taken place 'outside' itself. The moment we recognize what has turned into the structure of the schemas on the basis of which evidence appears to us as evidence, the hegemony of consciousness is destroyed. One of the meanings of that complex notion of the will to power is this. Far from being able to be summed up and centred in consciousness, or in the knowledge each of us has of himself and the responsibility each conceives for himself, the individual personality is an ensemble, perhaps not even a system, of different strata or 'pulsations' as we might call them (Nietzsche calls them 'passions') that are at odds with one another and give rise to equilibria that are never more than provisional.

On this view, the classical/Christian idea of the person derives its legitimacy solely from the fact that European man, driven by the pressures of social demands and the urge to productivity and domination, is organized and governed by consciousness, by reason, and by the 'passion for truth',[5] to which the other components of his personality are subordinated. Paradoxically, however, precisely through its own passion for truth and the pursuit of truth consciousness has brought itself into crisis. It has come to realize that it amounts to only one passion among many, that hegemony has been attained through more or less casual or at least external circumstances. Above all it has discovered that the subordinated passions have been anything but crushed: they avenge themselves for their humiliating condition in the way that slaves do on their master, by imposing on the very consciousness that believes it has them under control a distorted and degenerate logic of their own. (The topic is fascinatingly explored in *Beyond Good and Evil* and *The Genealogy of Morals*.)

45

This discovery leaves consciousness in a kind of intermediate position, the position defined as nihilism.[6] Consciousness grows aware that it has ceased to be the supreme
instance of personality. But learned Socratic ignorance is
then fundamentally subverted, since knowing that it does
not know, that it no longer constitutes the totality of the I,
now ceases to be a mark of conscious superiority. What
consciousness really fails to see is not the object in front of it,
but its own nature, its own constitution, its own hidden
origin, indeed why of its own 'choices' and of the evidence it
feels compelled to accept. Socratic reason, or the knowledge
of non-knowledge, was reason coming of age, and it is not
incidental that the concept of *Mündikeit* is so important in
Kant, precisely where reason becomes Socratically aware of
its own limitations and thus in a sense masters them.

Thus, testimony is unreliable in Nietzsche precisely insofar as it is given by an individual who is defined in terms of
the supremacy of consciousness over all other aspects of
personality. For, to use a juridical metaphor, this individual
has not come of age; he is not 'master' of himself. In fact, the
supremacy of consciousness, on the basis of which a person
answers for himself and gives testimony, is a fictitious
supremacy, undermined at the foundations by the hidden
revolt of the other passions, the revolt that gives birth to the
colossal display of neuroses that is our civilization. The
supremacy of consciousness is further undermined, again at
the level of neurosis by the awareness it has acquired of its
own 'superficiality'.

In this perspective, the Kierkegaardian apology for the
subjective thinker and existential *Angst*, together with their
subsequent developments in philosophy, look extremely
remote, like something still trapped within the framework of
the bourgeois/Christian tradition. And talk about testimony
seems to lose all its meaning. In fact, its subject vanishes.
The witness himself is reduced to the level of pure symptom.
Far from being the ultimate and active centre of interpreta-

tion, he turns into an object for subsequent interpretations.

I do not want to venture hypotheses in such a vast and constantly changing area of study as that which conceives of a possible relation between Nietzsche and psychoanalysis, whether it be historical/biographical or purely theoretical. I will merely note that Nietzsche's critique of the notion of the subject anticipates its actual destruction at the hands of analytical psychology in our own century. The notion of testimony goes 'out of date' as a result of the inversion of the traditional hierarchy of the elements of the individual psyche. This inversion has meant an increasingly dominant role for the unconscious, a tendency not unrelated to Nietzsche's stress on instinctive life.

What is generally referred to as Heidegger's *Kehre*, the abrupt ontological mutation in his thought after *Being and Time*, led to an analogous result, at least with respect to the critique of the notion of the subject. If Nietzsche's critique of the bourgeois/Christian subject anticipates and questions themes and arguments later developed by psychoanalysis, Heidegger's effort to overcome the idea of the subject has a more precisely ontological character, even if we must still ask what that may mean. The passage in *Holzwege* where (his linguistic obscurity for once fully justified) Heidegger calls for the overcoming of subjectivity as the constitutive feature of man[7] comes at the end of an itinerary that is of particular interest here, for it started from precisely the kind of existentialistic, Kierkegaardian and Augustinian positions that also provided the context for the emergence of the problematic of testimony.

If we leave aside *What is Metaphysics?* one of the most striking features of Heidegger's writings after *Being and Time* is the disappearance of a whole range of themes which had been extremely prominent both in his own early thought and even more so in the developments of it put forward by various existentialistic thinkers. Such themes include that of *Angst*, of course, but also authenticity (with its correlative of inauthenticity). In the absence of an explicit consideration of testimony in Heidegger, we must focus our discussion on the latter, to which testimony is closely related, especially in its philosophico-theological developments in existentialist circles. An elucidation of the connections involved here would obviously be a considerable undertaking, requiring a formal definition of testimony itself, which I have instead taken here in the 'average' and 'everyday' sense which is the starting-point for Heidegger's analysis in *Being and Time*. As I indicated at the start, testimony implies the idea of a constitutive relation between the individual and truth: on one hand, truth is someone's without ceasing to be truth; and on the other it is truth precisely and only insofar as it is the truth of *someone* who testifies to it. If this implication is validly drawn, the notion of testimony can be related to Heideggerian authenticity as contrasted with inauthentic existence in the world of the *they*. While the chatter of the inauthentic *they* touches on everything but relates to nothing, authenticity does not allow 'our fore-havings, foresight, and fore-conception' (constituting our precomprehension) 'to be presented to us by fancies and popular conceptions' (BT p. 195). Instead, it appropriates the thing itself. And because the thing in *Being and Time* is always an instrument, this appropriation is possible only insofar as the thing is taken up into a project decided on and chosen by Dasein; Dasein thus appropriates the thing only insofar as it appropriates itself, only insofar as it is authentic.[8]

There are for Heidegger two conditions for the attainment of truth, which he still seems to envisage here in terms of *adaequatio*. First, we have to have opted for our own most authentic possibility, and second, we have to be pursuing truth within a project that is the very existence of Dasein. This talk of 'opting' clearly implies that the project is radically individual, as is the decision that no one can take (and the death that no one can die) on my behalf.

Nevertheless, whether easily demonstrable or not, such analogies between Heidegger's idea of authenticity and the idea of testimony are not my main concern here. Rather, I want to show how and why the ontological turn in Heidegger's thought involves an intensification of his critique of the bourgeois/Christian idea of the subject. In fact, the suppression, indeed the complete disappearance of notions like that of authenticity in the later Heidegger is merely a symptom of this intensification. Already in *Being and Time* no moral significance could legitimately be sought in the authentic/inauthentic opposition, although it always implied a reference to the notion of decision; in the later works there seems to be no point in talking about a choice on man's part, unless it is the choice to 'wait' and 'prepare' for a new advent of Being. This becomes increasingly evident after the 'Letter on Humanism', where 'that which throws, in the project, is Being', and in the later thinking about language. But the underlying assumptions are already to be found in 'On the Essence of Truth', where man's freedom is rooted and founded in a deeper freedom, which then turns out to be the freedom of Being itself in its epochal essence.

In Heidegger, the disappearance of the idea of authenticity and the loss of the meaning of the subject go hand in hand with the deepening of his analysis of metaphysics as the destiny of Western thought, if not of human thought in general. Insofar as metaphysics is recognized as destiny, the distinction between authenticity and inauthenticity no longer occurs within the individual, but is rather an event that concerns Being itself and its 'structures'. Inauthenticity is the non-truth that necessarily accompanies and 'founds' truth as disclosedness. According to *Being and Time* Dasein is to be found always, already, primordially, in inauthenticity. In the ontological perspective that is later developed, this means that truth arises and is disclosed always and only in a setting of non-truth, of *epoché*, of suspension and concealment.

One result is that we lose an important distinction found in *Being and Time*, a distinction much stressed by the critics, especially the Marxist ones from Lukács onwards. In *Being and Time* the inauthenticity in which Dasein always, already and primordially exists is tied to the fact that Dasein exists with others, in society, and consequently always tends to take common opinion as the basis for its projects. But once metaphysics has been recognized as destiny, the individual's belonging to a historical world becomes a possibility that is constitutive. One does not become authentic by leaving the world of the *they* in a personal assumption of responsibility; entry into the sphere of authentic existence, which does not forget Being in its preoccupation with beings, can only occur (if it actually can) through the modification of this world, through the transformation of one epoch of Being into another.

It is not my concern here to explore all the consequences of this turn in Heidegger's thought. I shall not attempt for example, to decide whether this turn simply extends and universalizes the idea of inauthenticity, from which it becomes quite impossible for Dasein to escape (whereas *Being and Time* still allowed for the possibility of authentic decision). My point is this: the theory of metaphysics as the destiny of Being yields the discovery that belonging to a historical world is necessarily and unavoidably constitutive of individuality. There can be no individual authenticity in an inauthentic world; the move into authenticity depends on a comprehensive transformation of this world, on the inauguration of a different 'epoch of Being'.

I believe that acceptance of this fact not only allows the discovery of an important dimension of the significance of the crisis in the notion of the subject; it also sheds new light on the question of the *Kehre* in Heidegger's thought, accomplishing a synthesis of its various interpretations. In general there are two types of such interpretation; one is an 'internal' interpretation, tending to deny any fundamental break between the Heidegger of *Being and Time* and the later Heidegger. The other is a biographical/political interpretation, linking what is now held to be a clear relinquishment of the positions in *Being and Time* to its author's 'adherence' to Nazism.[9] Two types of consideration provide the best arguments for the 'internal' interpretation. First, there is the fact that *Being and Time* is from the outset frankly ontological in its concerns, insofar as its analysis of existence was to have served purely as a preparation for a rethinking of the problem of Being. Second, the starting-point of *Being and Time*, as well as the analysis in the published part of the work, were already orientated towards the negation of all possible transcendentalism, of all doctrines of 'the subject'. Consequently they were open to and indeed specifically moving towards an acceptance of the 'subject's' belonging to a sphere much broader than himself and his own decisions. In this light, Heidegger's intellectual itinerary after *Being and Time* contains another highly revealing element. Starting with a critique of Neokantian and phenomenological transcendentalism, in the name of exigencies that are existential in a broadly Kierkegaardian sense (for there is a profound analogy between Heidegger's polemic against Neokantianism and Kierkegaard's polemic against Hegel), Heidegger ultimately 'negates' and overcomes those same exigencies. The Christian/bourgeois individual is set over and against the transcendental subject; however, what the ontological *Kehre* ultimately demonstrates is that this individual shares the same characteristics as that 'subject', and that the critique of transcendentalism implies also a crisis for bourgeois/ Christian individuality. In other words, these two notions are very far from being opposed to each other in the radical manner suggested by the classical antithesis between Hegel and Kierkegaard, for they share the same roots. A negation of one cannot fail to lead to a negation of the other.

This is the line of interpretation which I have called 'internal'; it considers the *Kehre* to be foreshadowed both in

51

the questions that prompted it and in the provisional results of *Being and Time*. But this line can be contrasted with another one, exemplified above all by Löwith's polemical book, *Heidegger Denker in dürftiger Zeit*.[10] In this book the hiatus between *Being and Time* and the subsequent works is seen as so drastic that it cannot be explained except by reference to a biographical fact: Heidegger's adherence to Nazism. A more 'theoretical' variation of this interpretation can be found in the position of Lukács and Adorno,[11] where the Heidegger of *Being and Time* is linked with Nazism and the Heidegger of the ontological mutation with modern technocratic society. In both cases, and not on account of a 'biographical' fact, as in Löwith, intrinsic and structural reasons are adduced to justify the assessment of Heidegger's thought as an ideological mask, initially for the Fascism of the thirties, and then for the neocapitalistic Fascism of today.

Lukács's interpretation is far too bound up with the notion of inauthenticity in *Being and Time*, a notion that Heidegger himself subsequently surpassed. The criticisms put forward by Löwith and Adorno, however, have something in common. They attack Heidegger for having theorized the decline of the subject in the face of more powerful forces: historical destiny, or, in any event, Being. But it is precisely here that we find a basis for refuting such objections and polemical readings – at least in terms of their valuations, if not their content. For on one hand they effectively refute the objections of Lukács, while on the other they can easily be subsumed under what I have called the 'internal' interpretation of the *Kehre*.

That is, the real meaning of the ontological turn in Heidegger's philosophy after *Being and Time* lies in the recognition that the bourgeois/Christian idea of the subject is an inadequate one in which to interpret the historical experience of modern man. My approach does not deny the historical link between Heideggerian ontology and Nazism: it interprets it in a more radical fashion. Heidegger was not merely an apologist for Nazism; rather, it is simply that in the epoch of the formation of great 'integrated' states (European Fascist societies, Stalinist Russia, the monopolistic United States, etc. . .), he was acutely aware of the power that suprapersonal structures have over the individual, indeed more radically aware than anyone else, perhaps even more so than Marxist thinkers themselves. The *Introduction to Metaphysics* grasps the very root of the constitution of our civilization's conceptual language; in this respect it represents that very 'complement' which has been called for to fill the lacunae of Marx's *Capital*.[12] This might allow a rereading of the political writings and speeches from Heidegger's rectorship period, in which his admittedly equivocal approach to Nazism as 'destiny' may simply bear witness to his recognition of this *necessary* predominance of sociopolitical structures over individual ones in human experience. That Heidegger's thought fails to oppose suprapersonal 'forces' in the name of 'existential' or 'personal' needs and values (i.e. in the name of the Kierkegaardian individual) should not be seen as a limitation. Rather, this is the most positive and 'prophetic' dimension of his thinking, directed towards the understanding of new and hitherto unknown characteristics of experience.

Obviously, what matters here is not a demonstration of this reading of the *Kehre* in reference to philological and critical studies of Heidegger. This at least plausible reading serves only to suggest another important aspect of the crisis of the subject in contemporary thought. While the aspect represented by Nietzsche concerns the discovery of the stratiform character of the individual psyche and the importance of the unconscious, Heidegger represents the crisis of the subject in reference to its radical and constitutive belonging to a historico-social world. In all probability this also explains the importance of language in his thought.

These, I think, are the two crucial dimensions of the crisis of the bourgeois/Christian subject (and, earlier, the transcendental subject): the decline of the hegemonic role of consciousness (understood above all as self-consciousness) as regards both the other internal forces constituting a person and also the 'historical forces'. What new lines of development are opened up by this crisis of the subject? And what meaning can discourse about testimony possibly have in such a situation?

There are many indications in the theories of Nietzsche and Heidegger that development cannot, or should not, lead in the direction of an 'impersonalistic' ontology, exemplified, for example, in certain varieties of structuralism. The very fact that hermeneutical issues and the problem of language stand in the forefront of their thought cannot but mean that for them humans have a special position with regard to Being; in fact, Heidegger explicitly says so on more than one occasion. Likewise, the Nietzschean idea of the superman, providing it is not confused with some concept of 'hyperhumanity' in which the very features of bourgeois/Christian subjectivity it intends to negate are simply magnified to the nth degree, alludes at least to the fact that, even and especially in the world conceived as Will to Power, humans occupy a key position.

To pose the problem of testimony – however approximate the meaning of this term in the person-truth nexus – means to pose the problem, once the limits and the decline of the bourgeois/Christian subject have been acknowledged, of this special position occupied by humans. In other words, it means restating the problem of the meaning of action and historical choice. We have discovered that history *does not* play itself out on the level of our conscious individual decisions, whether because such decisions only mask and conceal decisions and choices already taken, of which we are unaware, though they guide us, or because what is at stake in those very decisions that we take to be our own is our belonging to a historical world, to a class, a language that conditions and *defines* us. And yet, these two sources of 'conditioning' are not on the same level.

hegemonic role of consciousness is framed and rooted in a conception of truth as a manner in which a certain form of life (which means certain relations of domination) conserves and empowers itself. This means that even in Nietzsche belonging to a historical world has fundamental importance, since the bourgeois/Christian personality itself, defined as it is in terms of the hegemony of consciousness, is a particular form of life called for by certain historical relations of domination. But again, this also means that the construction of the superman cannot be merely, or even primarily, the elaboration of a hermeneutical method that would allow us to lay bare our unconscious motives. Such a 'solution' to the problem would still be contained within the horizon of the bourgeois/Christian subject, the horizon of hegemonic self-consciousness. To construct the superman, in *Zarathustra*, means primarily constructing *his world*. The superman is not possible as a purely exceptional individual (if anything, this might be the *Freigeist*). He exists only insofar as he has a world. Moreover, such an existence is not born from the decision of any one individual, or from some individual conversion. It requires the preparation of generations.

Nietzsche's point here is analogous to Heidegger's stress on the fact that the new epoch of Being cannot depend on one of our decisions. The most we can do is wait for it and prepare for its coming (though *how* we do this is unclear). Two elements can be noted in both approaches. Firstly, truth does not amount to a 'true proposition' but rather to a general order of the world, a 'historical structure', a form of life, or an epoch of Being. Secondly, the inauguration of this new epoch does not depend on the individual and his or her decision, for only in such a new world could a person capable of such a decision be born. At most, the arrival of the new era and the birth of the decisive individual can only surface together.

This leads to the problem raised by Marx in his Third Thesis on Feuerbach. Having asserted the materialistic/mechanical doctrine concerning the decisive influence of circumstances and education on the individual, Marx adds as the doctrine's necessary complement that circumstances are themselves subject to modification by men. Marx seems not to have grasped the circularity of this process (which perhaps represents the truly demystified form of the hermeneutical circle). A glance at the First Thesis makes clear what he is trying to say: that Being which determines individual consciousness is not to be understood as object set against subject, for this Being is itself a historical product, heavily imbued with subjective and conscious connotations, a point made by Ernst Bloch in his commentary on the question.[13] If Being is not conceived as the opposite of consciousness or as an *objectum* placed before the subject, but as having a dialectical relation with it, a relation that has always already been initiated, then the solution to the circle (and this is the conclusion to Marx's Third Thesis) lies in revolutionary praxis, understood as 'the coincidence of environmental variations with human activity'.

This idea, as presented in the context of the *Theses* and with the meaning it possesses in the totality of Marx's thought, is relevant on two grounds to the problem I have been discussing, the problem, that is, of rediscovering the significance of testimony as the meaning of action and historical choice. First and foremost, it is relevant because the possibility of a revolutionary praxis is explicitly linked by Marx to the rejection of an 'objectivistic' conception of being. In turn, this suggests that certain critics have been justified in asserting that the reason why Heidegger finds it difficult to conceive of historical choice as possible or even significant has to do with the fact that his thought contains a residual metaphysical conception of Being.[14] To affirm that the initiative in history falls to Being rather than humans (although it must be borne in mind that Heidegger himself never explicitly speaks in these terms) means to continue to conceive of the man/being relation in terms of a subject/object opposition, something which is contrary to the deepest drift of Heidegger's thinking. In fact, the subject that in Heideggerian ontology is denied the possibility of any initiative is the bourgeois/Christian subject. Pessimism about the possibility of any significant historical action on the part of human beings remains within the horizon of this subject, to the extent that its decline is viewed as synonymous with the decline of humanity itself. The assumption is that the subjective mode of being is the only possible mode of human being, so that if the subject is denied then so is humanity.

The Marxian idea of revolutionary praxis seems to have something positive to say on this point as well. For Marx revolutionary action is of course not the work of an isolated individual but of a class. In fact, one of the clear messages of Marx's entire work is generally that the protagonists of history are not isolated individuals but classes. The bourgeois/Christian individual operates in the sphere of abstract concepts; perhaps the only individual is the Hegelian professor caricatured by Kierkegaard (although Hegel's own account is very different). The individual is the Cartesian of provisional morality, changing himself instead of trying to change the world. But certainly for Nietzsche and at least to some extent for Heidegger,[15] the move from inauthenticity to authenticity, or from non–truth to truth, is not merely a theoretical game of dice, transpiring in consciousness. It consists rather in the historical (and political) construction of a world, and in making this move the individual measures himself concretely against others, as allies or adversaries, and in both cases discovers and plumbs the reality of class.

Whether or not we accept Marxian terminology, the points made by Marx need to be borne in mind. After the decline of the subject, the only way to restore meaning to the notion of testimony, as well as to that historical action on the part of human beings to which the notion of testimony is tied, is to rid ourselves of all residual objectivism in our conception of Being. At the same time we must stop thinking of the bourgeois/Christian individual as the only possible subject of history and the only centre of initiative. And these requirements must both be satisfied at the same time; there must be no question of accepting only the second or of attributing the initiative in history solely to Being (as in Heidegger) or to some bureaucracy (as in neocapitalistic or communist technocracies), both of which confront the subject with the overbearing power of the object. This makes it possible for us to relate the Heideggerian affirmation of the undefinitiveness of the subject (in the passage I have alluded to in 'The Origin of the Work of Art') to other, analogous affirmations in Ernst Bloch's *The Principle of Hope*.[16] The discovery that the protagonist of history is not the individual but the class is just the first step on the way to the discovery, practical and theoretical at once, of a new and more authentic mode of human existence. For the time being it can be seen only in occasional and tantalizingly ambiguous glimmerings.

Notes

1 Cf. K. Jaspers, *The Perennial Scope of Philosophy*, trans. Karl Mannheim, London, 1950, p. 10.
2 F. Nietzsche, *Thus spoke Zarathustra*, trans. R. J. Hollingdale, Harmondsworth, 1969, p. 116; and *Twilight of the Idols/The Anti-Christ*, trans. R. J. Hollingdale, Harmondsworth, 1988, p. 171.
3 See e.g. *The Will to Power*, nos 533, 535, 539.
4 F. Nietzsche, *Twilight of the Idols/the Anti-Christ*, Harmondsworth, 1988, p. 170.
5 The whole of *The Will to Power* is the story of how the passion for truth has made itself constitutive of the form of life that is characteristic of European man: see e.g. nos 493, 498. See also the passage in the *Werke*, Musarion edition, vol. XIV, p. 176, where it is explicitly stated that the will to power has '*become* the strongest impulse' (the italics are Nietzsche's), and that this is the situation that faces

Zarathustra. See further the epilogue (1888) to *Nietzsche contra Wagner* in *The Portable Nietzsche*, New York, 1954).

6   On nihilism as an intermediate state, whose meaning is ambivalent, cf. *The Will to Power*, nos 10, 13, 22, 23, 585(B).

7   Cf. *The Question concerning Technology*, Part III, 'The Age of the World Picture', p. 152:

> In the planetary imperialism of technologically organized man, the subjectivism of man attains its acme, from which point it will descend to the level of organized uniformity and there firmly establish itself. This uniformity becomes the surest instrument of total, i.e. technological rule over earth. The modern freedom of subjectivity vanishes totally in the objectivity commensurate with it. Man cannot, of himself, abandon this destining of his modern essence or abolish it by a fiat. But man can, as he thinks ahead, ponder this: being subject as humanity has not always been the sole possibility belonging to the essence of historical man, which is always beginning in a primal way, nor will it always be.

8   On this whole topic see my own work *Introduzione a Heidegger*, Bari, 1971, ch. 1.

9   Documents from this period, including speeches and occasional writings, have been edited by C. Schneeberger in his *Ergänzungen zu einer Heidegger-Bibliographie*, Berne, 1960, and *Nachlese zu Heidegger*, Berne, 1962. As far as Heidegger's relations with Nazism are concerned, it is worth noting that after 1934 and his resignation from the rectorship, Heidegger took no further interest in politics and published virtually nothing more until the end of the War. Furthermore, it is highly significant that he devoted the years between 1935 and 1943 chiefly to working out an interpretation of Nietzsche in ·complete contradiction to the one favoured by Nazi propaganda.

10 *Heidegger Denker in dürftiger Zeit*, Frankfurt, 1953.

11 Cf. G. Lukács, *The Destruction of Reason*, London and Atlantic Highlands, NJ, 1981; T. Adorno, *The Jargon of Authenticity*,

trans. K. Tarnowski and F. Will, London, 1973; *Negative Dialectics*, trans. E. B. Ashton, New York, 1973.

12   Cf. the introduction to A. Sohn Rethel, *Intellectual and Manual Labour: A critique of epistemology*, London, 1978.

13   Cf. E. Bloch, *The Principle of Hope*, trans. N. Plaice, S. Plaice and P. Knight, Oxford, 1986, vol. I pp. 260–2.

14   One of the first to put forward this hypothesis was P. Furstenau, in his *Heidegger. Das Gefüge seines Denkens*, Frankfurt, 1958.

15   In this connection there is a relevant passage in Heidegger's essay on 'The Origin of the Work of Art', where he enumerates the various ways in which truth arises, i.e. the ways in which a new epoch of Being is opened. Significantly, political action is numbered among these ways and on the same grounds as poetry and thought. See Martin Heidegger, *Poetry, Language, Thought*, trans. A. Hofstadter, New York, 1971, ch. II p. 62.

16   Cf. Bloch, *The Principle of Hope*, vol. II p. 674.:

> Just as Marxism has discovered the really self-generating subject of history in working man, just as it only allows it to be discovered and to realize itself completely in socialist terms, so it is probable that Marxism will also advance in technology to the unknown, in itself not yet manifested subject of natural processes; mediating human beings with that subject, that subject with human beings and itself with itself.

3

Nietzsche and Difference

To raise the question of 'Nietzsche and difference' is simply to reconsider from a particular standpoint a more general issue that could be labelled as the problem of the relevance or irrelevance of Nietzsche. The choice of this standpoint is justified by the fact that it is precisely the contemporary philosophy of difference (an expression I shall expound hereafter) that has proved to offer a particularly fruitful and stimulating approach to Nietzsche. This is a consequence of the fact that the philosophy of difference was itself profoundly influenced and conditioned by Nietzsche long before it actually discovered him and explicitly singled him out as a historiographical problem. Thus there is a circularity that justifies this particular way of approaching the question. While the recognition of such a circularity makes sense from the hermeneutical point of view, it none the less leaves a tension between the contemporary philosophy of difference and Nietzsche; and my discussion will be situated within this tension or within the space opened by this specific 'difference'.

It will be no surprise that what I propose to call the philosophy of difference is to be understood principally in reference to Heidegger. Heidegger in turn is the thinker whose influence has been paramount in contemporary readings of Nietzsche; I am thinking not just of the two volumes of his *Nietzsche* (1961), but also of the earlier essays that partially anticipated the conclusions of these volumes, the ones published in *Holzwege*, *Vorträge und Aufsätze*, and *Was heisst Denken?* Difference plays a crucial role not simply in Heidegger's interpretation of Nietzsche but in the whole of his philosophy. Difference is of course an important issue in the introduction to *Being and Time*, a constitutive element of which is the programme for 'destructing' the history of ontology (see section 6). The primordial inspiration for the argument in *Being and Time* is the inadequacy of the notion of Being as handed down by metaphysics for the description and comprehension of what it pre-eminently is, namely, human existence and historicity. In *Being and Time*, it is not only man who raises the problem of Being insofar as he raises the question of the meaning of Being; but, more radically than this, it is man who problematizes the idea of Being as metaphysics has known and practised it, in that this idea does not 'apply' to a particularly human mode of being. However, *Being and Time* ultimately fails to replace a metaphysical conception of Being with a more adequate and comprehensive notion, capable of doing justice to the historicity of existence. Nor is this simply a result of the fact that *Being and Time* was never finished; even if Heidegger had been able to complete the whole work as outlined in the concluding paragraph of his introduction, he would not have succeeded in discovering a more satisfactory definition of the idea of Being. What *Being and Time* does show, however, is that Being as conceived by metaphysics – Being defined as pure and simple presence – *is given* within and as a moment of a horizon established as a 'temporal' event, not in the sense that it is a fact in time, but in the sense that it is the establishing of temporality itself as a unity of the three *ekstases*, the three dimensions of past, present and future. Now, this approach to the problem of Being, which neither gives nor can give rise to a 'definition' of Being, provides the basis for the philosophy of difference. In one sense difference already provides the starting-point for *Being and Time*, since to raise a question about the meaning of Being bears witness to the fact that such meaning is not given in beings as such. What *Being and Time* achieves from the point of view of the explicit theorization of difference is clearly summarized in *The Essence of Reasons*, written shortly after it in 1929:

> The unconcealment (*Unverborgenheit*) of Being is the truth of the Being *of* being, whether or not the latter is real. In the unconcealedness of being, on the other hand, lies a prior unconcealedness of its Being. Each after its own fashion, ontic and ontological truth, concern being in its Being and the *Being* of being. They belong together essentially, by reason of their relationship to the *difference* (*Unterschied*) *between Being and being* (*ontologische Differenz*). The essence of truth, which is and must be bifurcated ontically and ontologically, is only possible given this difference (ER pp. 26–7).

The difference Heidegger is talking about here is the one that always obtains between something that appears within a certain horizon and the horizon itself as an opening that makes possible the appearance of the being within it. As has been suggested, this difference is far from constituting a terminus for reflection or a place where thinking may settle. The only way it could be so is if, following the pattern set by forms of historicism and neokantianism, thinking contented itself with making ontological difference the methodological basis for a philosophy of culture, a philosophy which, guided by that notion, would be characterized by its capacity to insert the intellectual contents and products of the various historical manifestations of humanity into the horizon of their respective *epistemai*. In Heidegger the notion of difference does not move in this direction; rather, difference itself is foregrounded and problematized *as such*. This can be seen in the concluding paragraph of *Being and Time*, where the issue is raised as a question about why difference has been forgotten. The question asked by Heidegger there is this: if neither Dasein nor being-in-the-world are thinkable under the category of objectivity and pure presence, then 'why does Being get conceived "proximally" in terms of the present-at-hand? . . . *Why* does this reifying always keep coming back to exercise its dominion?'[1] Here the problem of ontological difference is not conceived in reference to what it differentiates or to the reasons and modalities of such differentiation. Rather, it may be translated into the question 'what about difference?' Here we might apply the well-known distinction between the subjective and the objective genitive which Heidegger draws in connection with the thought of Being in his 'Letter on Humanism' (BW pp. 194–6). The problem of difference is a problem concerning difference itself, rather than its terms and their reasons. In my view, one must insist on precisely Heidegger's way of stating the problem of difference: the reference to the subjective and objective genitive is more than a reference to a particular distinction on one page of Heidegger's text. It is not a *hapax legomenon* but a turn of thought constitutive of Heideggerian thinking on Being. It is also clear, for example, that the same genitive ambivalence applies to the expression the 'event of Being'. And, as we shall see, it is equally necessary to recognize this dual genitive even in the idea of metaphysics as the history or destiny of Being.

However, what I have called 'the philosophy of difference', inspired by Heidegger and prevalent today in a certain sector of French culture, tends to obscure and forget the various ways in which difference can be problematized. It can in general be accused of failing to absorb the suggestion made in the last paragraph of *Being and Time*, both in its narrow literal sense (why is difference forgotten?) and in its more general methodological sense (what about difference as such?). It tends instead to begin with the actual forgetting of difference, contrasting with that a type of thinking which strives rather to remember difference, rediscovering and presenting it in various ways, thereby aiming to position itself in some sense beyond 'metaphysics'. Here, I think, is one of the essential ways in which the philosophy of difference as practised by the French diverges from its original manifestation in Heidegger. For Heidegger, the problem of recollecting difference never becomes merely an *observation of* a difference between Being and being; it is always a recollection of the *problem of* difference, in both the subjective and the objective sense of the genitive.

This divergence in orientation with respect to difference is also evident in contemporary readings of Nietzsche. Although, as I have said, it is precisely in the context of the philosophy of difference that Nietzsche is most extensively recalled and discussed today, the Heideggerian interpretation of him has not been developed. French readings of Nietzsche focusing on difference and positioned in a broadly Heideggerian framework, take up a strong stand against the Heideggarian view of him. And this, as we shall see, is a function of their different way of raising and comprehending the problem of difference.

It is well known that Heidegger does not consider Nietzsche a thinker of difference, since it is in Nietzsche's thought that we find the total accomplishment and unfolding of metaphysics, or the thinking that has forgotten Being and its difference from being. The metaphysical process is one in which there finally remains 'nothing to Being as such' (N vol. iv, p. 201) which is certainly the outcome of the Nietzschean idea of the will to power, or, as Heidegger renders it, the will to will. If such a reading is taken literally – and it implies a substantive homogeneity between Nietzsche and Platonism (against which Nietzsche thought he was rebelling) as well as between Nietzsche and Hegel – then the possible nexus between Nietzsche and difference can only be a negative one. Nietzsche will represent the phase of thought in which difference is most completely obscured. Only in this sense will Nietzsche also represent a turning-point, for as the culmination of metaphysics he also becomes the end of metaphysics and heralds, unwittingly and problematically, its overcoming.

But as I have suggested, especially in France, readings of Nietzsche generally inspired by Heidegger and by the question of difference have for the most part run *counter* to the letter of Heidegger's interpretation of Nietzsche. Writing in 1966, Derrida alleged that Heidegger could characterize Nietzsche as the culmination of metaphysics and Platonism only by a *mauvaise foi* equal to his lucidity and rigour.[2] It is not simply that, as Derrida observes, the annexation of his opponent to the history of metaphysics, and thus to the history of reified, representative and inauthentic thought, could just as well be done to Heidegger himself. The French critic goes on to make the much more precise point that one of the key elements in Nietzschean thought, the doctrine of tragedy and its twofold Dionysian and Apollonian 'principles', is in actual fact a supreme form of recollection of difference. In the closing pages of 'Force and Signification' (1963) he writes: 'If we must say, along with Schelling, that "all is but Dionysus", we must know . . . that, like pure force, Dionysus is worked by difference.'[3] The reference to Schelling is not crucial to the argument; what is fundamental here is the allusion to Nietzsche and the Dionysus–Apollo pairing, which is not interpreted as a primordial polarization but as a 'metaphorical' expression of a primordial difference internal to Dionysus himself (which certainly fits Nietzsche's own greater emphasis on Dionysus). This is a point that has been taken up by those French students of Nietzsche who look more or less explicitly to Derrida as well as to Heidegger. It should be noted, however, that in this part of Derrida, as indeed in the whole of his thought, the affirmation that all is only Dionysus, and that Dionysus is worked by difference, can only be regarded from a Heideggerian point of view as a metaphysical thesis. Moreover, at the point in Derrida to which we have been referring, there is a statement on the topic that seems quite explicit: 'The divergence, the *difference* between Dionysus and Apollo, between ardour and structure, cannot be erased in history, for it is not *in* history. It too, in an unexpected sense, is an original structure; the opening of history, historicity itself.'[4] From this point of view, the philosophy of difference is distinguished from metaphysical thought to the extent that instead of thinking Being as the fullness of presence, as stability and unity, it thinks it and enunciates it as difference, divergence, torment.

When in 1968 Derrida introduced his variant of *difference* he was being perfectly consistent with the positions he had taken in these earlier essays. But I do not at this point wish to apply my argument to Derrida himself and his elaboration of the idea of difference in that 1968 lecture. Rather, I should like to examine how the Derridean interpretation of difference, taken to suggest a vision of Being as no longer marked by fullness but by fracture and deficiency, has inspired further recent readings of Nietzsche in French thought, and in particular those of Bernard Pautrat, Jean Michel Rey and Sarah Kofman.[5] I shall pay special attention to the work of Pautrat, which seems to me the most substantial and significant as far as my own argument is concerned. It is Pautrat in particular who has suggested a response to the question I have raised about the metaphysical nature of the thesis according to which 'everything is only Dionysus etc.' Staying very close to Derrida, Pautrat distinguishes the metaphysical character of a proposition less in reference to the general significance it claims to have as affirming something about Being in its totality, than in terms of the type of relation established between language and its 'object'. The proposition 'all is nothing but Dionysus' is not explicitly discussed by Pautrat in these terms, but if we take it as an example, the thing that would make it quite undeniably non-metaphysical would also and above all be the name Dionysus. This would be true in two closely connected senses. First and foremost,

Dionysus is 'difference', fracture, mobility, etc. In the second place, Dionysus is a mythological name, marking out a semantic area that is irreducible to metaphysical, representative thought. In Nietzsche's text the name of Dionysus does not stand for something else, it is not some kind of allegory or symbol that is translatable into purely conceptual terms. In general we can say that Nietzsche's whole poetic and prophetic manner of writing, in which metaphor constantly eludes exhaustive decoding, exploits a way of relating signifier to signified that places it completely outside the ambit of the metaphysical mentality, dominated as that is by representationality. In other words, the fact that Nietzsche writes in a philosophical/poetic language in which a central importance can be attributed to a mythological figure like Dionysus is neither merely accidental nor a matter of pure stylistic preference. This language embodies a mode of being of discourse that 'corresponds' (although the term seems indispensable, I must point out that this is precisely the problem) to ontological difference. Thus a thesis like 'all is nothing but Dionysus' may look like a metaphysical one in that it is still a general proposition about Being, which it no longer considers as fullness and presence, but as difference and torment; but we should not attribute any importance to that. For thinkers like Derrida and his followers the crucial thing is that the use of the name Dionysus immediately places discourse in a zone other than that of metaphysics. Dionysus is neither a 'concept' nor a 'being' in the sense of something that is given in presence, in the sensible world or in the world of ideas and essences. And to say it is a 'poetic image' – conceiving of that expression outside the customary contrast between the objective knowledge of science and philosophy and poetry's world of 'purely imaginary' images – is to assert for it a relation to its signified that does not fit into the representative schemas of metaphysics, those that Heidegger analyses and describes, for example, when he reconstructs the genesis of the idea of truth as adequation or of 'objectivity' or 'object', and so on.

However, we are still left with the problem of how to give a positive account of the signifying–signified relationship set up in a poetic/philosophical text such as Nietzsche's. Even more important is the problem of clarifying the terms in which the relation of this text to difference is to be described. It should not be forgotten that what we are looking for here are the elements that allow Derridean readings to contrast Nietzsche as thinker of difference with the Heideggerian Nietzsche, the last of the metaphysicians and the last of the Platonists. Given that the Nietzschean text really cannot be read as a metaphysical nor even as a 'purely' poetic text in the ordinary sense of the word, in what sense does its peculiar poetic/philosophical quality represent a way of recollecting that difference which metaphysical discourse has always forgotten? A little way back I spoke provisionally of the language of Nietzsche 'corresponding' better to Being as difference, but this term cannot pass without discussion, for if it were taken literally it would still imply a mimetic relation between discourse and Being as 'object'. It is no accident that in the essay mentioned above on *Différance* and in various other places[6] Derrida freely admits that the introduction of the idea of difference is a 'throw of the dice', a game, an arbitrary decision that cannot be legitimized by reference to a state of things that could offer verification of it. The throw of the dice does not so much 'correspond' to difference, rather, it *practises* it. There is something analogous to this in the readings of Nietzsche I mentioned at the start, especially those of Pautrat and Rey. In refusing to describe Being in conceptual terms as something given in a settled manner outside discourse, the poetic/philosophical language used by Nietzsche recognizes and practises difference as something internal to discourse itself. Making use of ideas from Saussure, Derrida sees the signified as a fact of the signifier, a game of language, something that occurs as a product of differences internal to discourse. Nietzsche is not a 'philosopher who expresses himself through images'. What underlies the peculiar status of his text is the desire to inaugurate another mode of being for the word over against the 'thing'. One of the doctrines of *The Will to Power* is, of course, that what to the realist or positivist mentality are 'facts' are actually of an interpretative nature. There are no facts, only interpretations.[7] Nietzsche's philosophical/poetic text is the actual practice of this 'theory'. His text would be self-contradictory if it tried to present itself as theory, as an objective description and contemplation of a state of things.

But why is this way of conceiving and practising the signifier–signified relation to be viewed as a thought that recollects difference, and thus as post-metaphysical? In poetic discourse metaphor presents itself as such,[8] which means that the signified reveals itself as being actually produced by the play of the signifier. Thus difference, which is primordially manifested as the contrast between signifier and signified, is no longer taken for granted, accepted as already having happened, as a stable framework within which we stand but which we do not question. Taking up and elaborating another Heideggerian doctrine, that of the struggle between world and earth in the work of art,[9] difference is recollected in poetic language because there it is 'at work', whereas allegedly 'objective' theory assumes it as an indisputable fact that is always already given.

The meaning attributed by this interpretation of Nietzsche to the recollection of difference is as follows: difference is recollected to the extent that it is 'put into effect' in Nietzsche's text and in the philosophy of difference in general. Difference is not a pure and simple content of discourse; discourse recalls difference to the extent that it practises difference; it is a moment in which difference occurs. At the same time, what makes Nietzsche's poetic/ philosophical discourse an occurrence of difference ultimately relates to a particular repetitive character inherent in the discourse itself. Here recollection is taken literally. Of course it is true that in poetry the signifier is liberated from the terroristic domination of the signified and actually produces the signified as the effect of its own play; but from the structural point of view this event remains the same. The game is ever new, but the rules are established once and for all. They are the rules of that 'structure which is primordial in an unusual sense', as Derrida puts it, the structure that is difference. In the play of the signifier the primordial differentiation constantly recurs. The poetic event is not completely new; it only appears so in relation to 'serious' types of discourse, which derive their seriousness by starting from difference as already open, by taking it seriously, while the poet for ever reinstitutes it. But this reinstitution is in fact a restitution: on the one hand it restores differences that are other than the existing ones only in respect of 'content'; on the other it re-establishes difference in its condition as primordial event, forgotten as such by objectifying thought.

Of course this recollection of difference conceived on the model of repetition finds its legitimation in the Nietzschean doctrine of eternal recurrence, which these interpreters read in fact as no more than a theory of repetition. They buttress their reading with frequent references to Freud and to the meaning that analytical therapy seems to attribute to the repetition of a 'primal scene', such as the trauma that underlies neurosis or that of parental coitus, a scene, however, that is only 'primal' in appearance, since it too repeats another.[10] But can a thought or a discourse which is a 'repetition' or 'performance' of difference legitimately claim to be a recollection of difference which escapes from the sphere of representative thought characterized by the slavery of signifier to signified? Indeed, is such a thought of repetition what Nietzsche really had in mind? Both these questions are relevant, not only the first. The problems thrown up by the second question will have a decisive part to play in the way the first is resolved. In fact we do have every right to consider Nietzsche a thinker of difference, as long as we realize that this will mean making essential revisions of that which is presented as the philosophy of difference.

71

To begin with, the terms 'repetition' and 'performance' (especially the latter), as used by scholars like Pautrat and Rey, merit consideration for their closeness (even if only terminological) to representation. Nothing is more of a representation than a 'performance'. If in addition we consider the way that someone like Pautrat talks about the explicitly parodistic nature of Nietzsche's discourse with regard to metaphysics,[11] or describes it as a self-conscious and deliberate play of metaphor, the niggling suspicion of representativeness seems to be confirmed. In fact another typical figure of metaphysical discourse resurfaces here – consciousness as the self-consciousness of the 'subject' in front of its 'objects'. The archstructure of difference takes the place of the signified, of the Platonic idea, of the *ontos on* of all metaphysics: human discourse cannot unfold except in difference, either by forgetting it and taking it for granted as a natural framework or else by constantly repeating it in poetic discourse. Even if this other way of thinking is not said to be 'better' than the first – for this would then necessitate justifying such a 'superiority', and that can only be done within the horizon of adequation – it is in fact assumed to be so. The liberating significance attributed by such interpreters to the recollection, repetition and performance of difference is shown by the parallels so frequently drawn in their readings, not only between Nietzsche and Freud but also between Nietzsche and the critique of political economy in Marx. But if that thinking which remembers difference has some sort of (however carefully defined) 'superiority' over thinking which forgets difference, this superiority can be understood only in reference to the value of consciousness, to knowing subjectivity. Shades of Spinoza? At least in this precise and implicit sense, yes. But it would probably be much more appropriate to draw parallels with those models of 'palaeoexistentialistic' thought which retain a persistent hold on French culture. Thus, for example, another of the leading recent French interpreters of

Nietzsche is Maurice Blanchot, whose readings[12] seem much closer to Jaspers than to Heidegger. In short, it is difficult to see how a recollection of difference understood as performance and repetition can fail to depend on the existentialist illustration of (and apologia for) the finitude of the human condition, brought up to date, perhaps, through the recent discoveries of structural linguistics.[13]

If, as would need to be sustained more at length, the philosophy of difference inspired by Derrida's development of Heidegger is ultimately related to these models of early existentialism, it is not easy to see what Nietzsche could have in common with it. Nothwithstanding all those frequently illuminating observations on the anti-metaphysical significance of the peculiar language of the Nietzschean text, the only conceivable point of contact would be a view of Being that no longer understands it as fullness, presence or foundation, but rather as fracture, absence of foundation, work and pain. These turn out to be precisely the elements in Nietzsche that have clear origins in Schopenhauer, and they are perfectly homogeneous (as in Schopenhauer) with the metaphysical tradition in Heidegger's sense. Nor is it any accident that those interpreters of Nietzsche who draw their inspiration from Derrida lay such stress in their writings on Nietzsche's early works, which are precisely the ones where Schopenhauer is, of course, still powerfully present. By contrast, when critics like Pautrat, Rey and Kofman approach Nietzsche's mature thought and later doctrines – the superman, the will to power, eternal recurrence – their readings seem much less clear and convincing.

These happen to be the very doctrines in which we see at his most imposing the Nietzsche of the *ueber*, the Nietzsche of that overcoming which cannot readily be trapped in a philosophy of finitude. Moreover, the idea of eternal recurrence, the great message that is so fundamental to *Zarathustra*, as indeed to all Nietzsche's later works, seems to me to resist a reading of repetition such as that advanced by the French. In pointing to a mode of being no longer worked by the separation between essence and existence, event and meaning, and to a mode of existing that is no longer marked by the Oedipal conflict,[14] this doctrine seems to be at an opposite pole from the repetition or performance of difference as the recollection of a rupture that can never be overcome because it is the archstructure that founds and opens history itself. If anything, the very irreconcilability of eternal recurrence with the notion of history as developed and passed down in Western thought should convince us that what Nietzsche has in mind is precisely the demolition of such a structure of history, the one opened and founded by difference. Hence, it ought to convince us that eternal recurrence, far from consisting in the repetition and performance of difference, actually amounts to the end of history as dominion of difference.

Does this mean that on this point we must agree with Heidegger? Must we believe that Nietzsche deals with difference only in a negative way, insofar as his thought bears witness to the ultimate terminus reached by that metaphysical thought which identifies Being with beings? I believe there is a third way, though, strictly speaking, it is not another alternative but can rather be found in Heidegger's own thought, if the dialogue initiated by him with Nietzsche is taken to its logical conclusion. The argument that Nietzsche is not a thinker of difference, as Derrida and the French are, and that therefore Heidegger is right to see his thought as the supreme moment in the metaphysical forgetting of difference, suggests that even Heidegger's conception of difference is the same as that of Derrida and his followers. And yet the fact is that Heidegger never wrote and almost certainly never could have written a proposition like Derrida's 'all is nothing but Dionysus etc.' He was all too well aware that difference cannot be recollected if one continues to think it metaphysically as the 'structure' (even in an unusual sense) of the 'all'. Heidegger presents the question of how there may be a recollective thought and what it may be in a much more subtle and complex fashion and, moreover, fails to resolve the issue. It is here that we need to look for the root of the dissatisfaction we feel at his interpretation of Nietzsche, despite the fact that this interpretation is much more convincing and philosophically alive than Derridean readings. Essentially, Heidegger seems to read Nietzsche with much more sensitivity to the 'overcoming' dimension that Nietzsche wished to attribute to his own philosophy. But there remains something perplexing and unsatisfactory in Heidegger's conclusions about Nietzsche representing the greatest distance from Being and difference, as the final blind alley of metaphysics, as proclaiming a new epoch only negatively and unconsciously. I believe that all this has to do with the still open question of what Heidegger meant by recollective thought. Is it a thought which, unlike metaphysics and its identification of Being with beings, rediscovers, makes present, or perhaps even repeats and performs the primordial act in which Being opens the horizon within which beings can appear, i.e. Being as different(iating) difference? In other words, does this thought indeed resemble Derrida's in that it no longer thinks of Being as fullness and presence, but as labour and absence of ground? If this were so, it would not be clear why Heidegger finds the problem of overcoming metaphysics so difficult; its solution does not depend on man, for it can only be prepared for as something far in the future, by means of more or less passive listening and waiting. However difficult, or perhaps even impossible, it may be to say what recollective thought means for Heidegger, we can at least see what it is not. He is certainly not talking about recalling difference for the sake of obtaining a firmer grasp of the historicity of cultural horizons in their 'eventual' character; nor about recalling difference in order to settle into it through a thought that is ultimately shaped as an exercise in finitude, the at once insuperable and constitutive finitude of the human condition.

On the positive side, we may also note that where Derrida speaks of difference, Heidegger prefers to speak of the selfsame (*das Selbe*), of that sameness which renders possible that *Gespräch* which we are insofar as we are human. This is how he puts it in his lecture on 'Hölderlin and the essence of poetry'.[15] Even so, it is clear that we cannot explore the meaning of recollection except with reference to the problem of overcoming metaphysics. It would seem to be legitimate to interpret Heidegger's whole development after *Being and Time* as an increasingly rigorous elucidation of the *eventual* nature of Being (to be understood in reference to Heidegger's stress on *Ereignis*, event, with all the implications that may be drawn from its etymological resonances). In *Being and Time*, with its separation of existentials from categories (the latter applying to the beings within the world, the former to Dasein, to humans), Heidegger has already abandoned any attempt to view man as definable in terms of nature, essence or stable structures. In his subsequent works this feature of existence is more and more explicitly linked to the eventuality of Being. This eventuality, which Heidegger also expresses through a stress on the verbal character inherent in the term *Wesen*, essence, signifies that everything we see as a structure, for example, the essence of truth as conformity of the proposition to the thing, is an event, an institution, a historical aperture of Being (or a historial one, in the sense of *Geschehen*). The history of Western metaphysics, of which Nietzsche appears here as the accomplishment, is in this sense the history of Being; it is the arising of a given epoch of Being, one dominated by mere presence at hand, by the ideal of objectivity, by language as a pure tool for communication. Is it therefore also an epoch of difference?

This question is the key to relaunching the Heideggerian interpretation of Nietzsche and also to opening up a dialogue with Heidegger's own thought. Would not the eventuality of Being also inevitably involve the archstructure of difference in its historicizing and eventualization of all structures?

To deny that the archstructure of difference is eventual would be equivalent to acknowledging that there cannot be any overcoming of metaphysics, for difference would be at the bottom of every opening of Being, every epoch, all history. But in that case it would function first and foremost as metaphysical stability; it would be only another name for the Platonic *ontos on*. In the second place there would be no history except as a constantly renewed repetition of the differentiation between Being and beings, and consequently as a repetition of the metaphysical forgetting of difference. The Heideggerian texts seem to be explicit in their claim that the epoch of metaphysics is not just one event among others that may occur in the framework of the archstructure of difference. Ontological difference is that particular feature of Being in virtue of which Being hides as it lets beings appear; the non-fortuitous result of this giving/concealing is metaphysics itself, and this is the sense in which metaphysics is the destiny and history of Being. However, this seems to mean that the disclosedness/concealment connection takes on a structural consistency and eludes the eventualization of all structures that Heidegger seeks. It amounts to saying that *there is*, in a quite settled fashion, a Being that is characterized as an ever-renewed co-involvement of disclosedness with concealment. This mistake Heidegger himself does not always seem to have avoided, and it underlies many of today's neoplatonizing and theologizing interpretations of his philosophy. But suppose we were to take the eventuality of Being seriously, suppose we were to read the expression 'metaphysics as the history of Being'[16] in its strongest sense, the sense that springs from making the genitive objective or *also* objective? Metaphysics would then be called the history or destiny of Being because Being itself belongs totally to metaphysics and to its history; not only the end of metaphysics, but the overcoming of metaphysics, which Heidegger sees himself as having to prepare for, would then be equivalent both to the end of Being and the end of ontological difference. What happens in Nietzsche, then, namely, that 'nothing remains of Being', would be the overcoming of metaphysics through the elimination of the very idea of Being. Could it be that the difficulties and the vague sense of 'marking time' peculiar to Heidegger's thought derive from the fact that the conception of the end of metaphysics as a veritable decline of Being involves a rather more extensive upheaval than the one we manage to conceive when we speak of the forgetfulness of Being and of ontological difference? In this view, what Heidegger calls a forgetting of ontological difference would no longer be the forgetting of the fact that Being is not identifiable with beings but the forgetting of difference as a problem, that is, of difference in its eventuality, the forgetting of why difference is established.

Metaphysics is the history of difference both insofar as it is governed and made possible by difference, and because difference is given and subsists only within the horizons of metaphysics. From this point of view, forgetting difference does not mean losing sight of the fact of difference: it means forgetting difference as a fact. This is not a failure to keep in mind *that* difference does actually dominate and condition *our* historical existence; it is to forget the question 'why difference?' Any fresh attempt to raise the issue of a deep affinity between Heidegger and Nietzsche will need to start from a reading of difference and recollection something like the one I have (admittedly sketchily) outlined here.

Let us leave open the possible development and 'demonstration' of this particular interpretative thesis as regards Heidegger, the question, in other words, of whether it is possible to read Heidegger's recollection of difference as also a straining to overcome difference itself, coincident with both overcoming metaphysics and the decline of Being. The main lines of such an interpretation of Heidegger are those I have sketched above: the eventual character of Being makes it impossible to view its own eventuality, and hence difference, as an archstructure valid for *all* possible history; the expression 'metaphysics as history of Being' is to be taken in both senses of the genitive. Being is not something or someone that *has* a history with which it is not completely identified; it belongs entirely to metaphysics; metaphysics is its history because it is only in metaphysics that Being is given, happens, eventualizes itself. Recollective thought thus acquires a less factual and less representative nature. The issue is not that of making difference present, coming to a realization of it, or 'becoming aware of it'. What Heidegger is interested in is rather recalling it in its character as event, an event eventualized within the horizon of the history of metaphysics. The difficulty for thinking which reaches these limits is not that 'technical' difficulty of constantly rediscovering difference beneath the masks laid on it by metaphysics. The fact is that it is not sufficient to remember or become aware of the difference between Being and beings; we also have to problematize it in its eventuality; the difficulty is that this requires us to be placed beyond the horizon of metaphysics, within which we belong by virtue of our very constitution. The only one who might truly achieve such an *Ueberwindung* would be the Nietzschean *Uebermensch*.

Recollection is also alluded to by Nietzsche, for example in aphorism 292 of *Human, all too Human*,[17] and even more in number 82 in 'The Wanderer and his Shadow':

An affectation on departing. – He who wants to desert a party or a religion believes it is incumbent upon him to refute it. But this is a very arrogant notion. All that is needed is that he should be clear as to the nature of the bonds that formerly tied him to this party or religion and to the fact that they no longer do so: that he should understand what kind of outlook impelled him to them and that it now impels him elsewhere. We did *not* attach ourselves to this party or religion *on strictly rational grounds*; we ought not to *affect* to have done so when we leave it.

79

If we are to understand the alternative represented by Nietzsche with respect to the recollection of difference as outlined in French thought and, more problematically, in Heidegger, then this aphorism (despite its lack of explicit reference to recollection) and the one cited in note 17, are both crucial. Nietzsche understands recollection as a way of relating to a past that is finished with and left behind, to paths we shall never go down again. In another text he uses the expression 'feasts of memory', celebrated by man at the end of metaphysics with respect to such spiritual forms of the past as art.[18] But there definitely remains a more Heideggerian element in Nietzsche alongside this joyful acknowledgement of how we were and how we are no longer: this is the element described in those aphorisms in *The Gay Science* that speak of the death of God.[19] God is dead, and this means that metaphysics and difference are over, but the full liberating potential inherent in this event will not enter the consciousness of humanity for centuries yet. Heideggerian recollection, which always revolves around difference as a problem (why and how difference was established and consolidated in the shadow of forgetting, how and in what sense it can decline with the end of metaphysics) is entirely located within the space of the interval spoken of by Nietzsche. The fascination, the suggestiveness and the relevance of Heideggerian thought are all explicable by the fact that we always find ourselves *de facto* in this interval, in this *Zwischen*. It is to recollection of this type that all those Nietzschean thoughts belong in which difference predominates as a vision of Being as labour, struggle or disequilibrium, those aspects to which Derrida alluded in talking about Dionysus, for example, the vision of history as the history of domination and power relations as developed in works like *The Genealogy of Morals* and *Beyond Good and Evil*.

This type of thought is still situated in a logic of force, as is shown by an unpublished fragment from the Zarathustra period[20] where Nietzsche speaks of 'transforming men by force' so that they can accept the new doctrine. But over against this there stands all the dancing thought of Zarathustra and recollection in the spirit of one who has taken his leave. The very question 'why difference?' still lingers within the logic of metaphysics, for one of the ways, or perhaps *the* way (although there are not so many, and it is always the same event) in which difference opens up between Being and beings, and in which metaphysical forgetting is prepared for, is as an opposition between foundation and 'founded'. That is why the recollection that affects no reasons for taking leave is the model for thinking that is no longer metaphysical but which truly 'overcomes'.

Zarathustra has taken his leave of metaphysics, of difference, of Being itself. Thus it is only partly legitimate to read the thought of Nietzsche/Zarathustra in terms of difference, focusing on the 'differential' character that seems to be implicit in the idea of the will to power. For on one hand in Nietzsche there always still remains by the side of the thought which has taken its leave another thought which dwells in the *Zwischen* between the death of God and the actual unfolding of extrahuman liberation. And on the other hand in the world of the superman as we try to think it here, the world in which nothing remains of Being, difference or metaphysics, there must still after all be history. This history, however, cannot be anything but a history of 'pure differences', as Nietzsche seems to suggest in the texts where he describes the will to power as essentially the will to impose interpretative perspectives, rather than a struggle for values, objects or positions of domination (and thus less than ever for 'power'). The world of the liberated signifier, of symbols posited and removed in the freedom of a great artistic creation (*ein sich selbst gebärendes Kunstwerk*),[21] will of course still be life, change, and in this sense history.

None the less, what probably lies concealed in this striving to rediscover even in the world of the superman, or of liberated humanity, that cherished difference which is the opening of *our* history, of history as we have so far lived it, as humanity has lived it in such bloody fashion right up till today, is the ancient fear of the end of history. Given that history as we know it and live it is the history of difference (between Being and beings, signifier and signified, slave and master, father and son) it would seem that the extra-metaphysical and extra human world as prophesied by Nietzsche has no history and therefore no life. The thought of the *Zwischen*, of the interval, the Heideggerian recollection of difference as a problem also responds to this fear, this need to remain forever in difference. Prophetically and utopianly, Nietzsche 'went beyond'. At the same time he left open the question of how to live and practise at one and the same time the dancing thought of Zarathustra and the recollection of difference that in part still accepts its logic and remains within it: 'the consciousness that I am dreaming and that I must go on dreaming' as the aphorism in *The Gay Science* has it.[22] Or, to use the Brechtian formula: 'we / who wanted to prepare the ground for friendliness / Could not ourselves be friendly.'[23] But all the same, not even Brecht was fully convinced that in the meantime, in the *Zwischen*, we could fail to be perfectly friendly.

Notes

1 BT p. 487.
2 In *Writing and Difference*, trans. A. Bass, London, 1978, p. 281.
3 Ibid., pp. 28–9.
4 Ibid., p. 28.
5 B. Pautrat, *Versions du soleil. Figures et système de Nietzsche*, Paris, 1971; J. M. Rey, *L'Enjeu des signes. Lecture de Nietzsche*, Paris, 1971; S. Kofman, *Nietzsche et le métaphore*, Paris, 1972.
6 'Différance' in *Margins of Philosophy*, trans. A. Bass, Brighton, 1982, pp. 7, 11 and *passim*; also, for example,

Positions, trans. A. Bass, London, 1981.

7 *The Will to Power*, no. 481.

8 Cf. S. Kofman, *Nietzsche et le métaphore*, pp. 137–9.

9 As is well known, this doctrine is treated in depth in 'The Origin of the Work of Art', written in 1936.

10 Cf. B. Pautrat, *Versions du soleil*, p. 147.

11 Ibid., pp. 290–1.

12 See, for example, *L'Entretien infini*, Paris, 1969, pp. 201–55.

13 The thesis that Derridean thought is ultimately still 'theological' is argued very effectively in a fine study by M. Dufrenne, 'Pour une philosophie non-théologique', published as the introduction to the second edition of *Le poétique*, Paris, 1973.

14 On this question the reader is referred to the discussion of the idea of eternal recurrence in my *Il soggetto e la maschera. Nietzsche e il problema della liberazione*, Milan, 1979.

15 This lecture was delivered in 1936 and published in *Erläuterungen zu Hölderlins Dichtung*, 1944. English translation in M. Heidegger, *Existence and Being*, London, 1949, pp. 291–315.

16 This is the title of one of the sections in Heidegger's *Nietzsche*, vol. II, p. 399 (*Die Metaphysik als Geschichte des Seins*).

17 HATH aphorism 292:

> *Forward.* – And with that, forward on the path of wisdom with a bold step and full of confidence! However you may be, serve yourself as your own source of experience! Throw off discontent with your nature, forgive yourself your own ego, for in any event you possess in yourself a ladder with a hundred rungs upon which you can climb to knowledge. The age in which with regret you feel yourself thrown counts you happy on account of this good fortune; it calls you to participate in experience that men of a later age will perhaps have to forgo. Do not underestimate the value of having been religious; discover all the reasons by virtue of which you have still had a genuine access to art. Can you not, precisely with aid of these experiences, follow with greater understanding tremendous stretches of the paths taken by earlier mankind? Is it not

on precisely *this* soil, which you sometimes find so displeasing, the soil of unclear thinking, that many of the most splendid fruits of more ancient cultures grew up? One must have loved religion and art like mother and nurse – otherwise one cannot grow wise. But one must be able to see beyond them, outgrow them; if one remains under their spell, one does not understand them. [. . .] Turn back and trace the footsteps of mankind as it made its great sorrowful way through the desert of the past: thus you will learn in the surest way whither all later mankind can and may not go again.

18 Cf. *Human, all too Human*, p. 223.
19 See in particular aphorism 343; but cf. also nos. 108 and 125.
20 This may be found in the Musarion edition of Nietzsche's *Werke*, vol. XIV, p. 179.
21 *The Will to Power*, no. 796.
22 *The Gay Science*, trans. W. Kaufmann, New York, 1974, no. 54.
23 Bertolt Brecht, *Poems*, edited by J. Willet and R. Manheim, London, 1976, p. 32. ('To those born late – ').

4

The Will to Power as Art

A very important feature of the contemporary debate about Nietzsche, particularly in France and Italy, is the way the Heideggerian interpretation of Nietzsche's concept of the will to power is used. Happily the cruder Nazi reading of this concept has gone out of fashion, and the interpretation set out in Heidegger's individual essays and his 1951 book on Nietzsche has answered a real need in Nietzsche criticism. The fact is that earlier non-Nazi readings before Heidegger never really came conclusively to grips with the idea of the will to power. This is certainly true of Löwith and Jaspers, whose writings are basic landmarks for the reading of other aspects of Nietzsche's thought. But it is Heidegger who provides a convincing and coherent contextualization for this problematic concept by framing it within his reading of Nietzsche as the culmination and end of metaphysics. Heidegger, of course, holds that metaphysics is that history at the end of which nothing is left of Being as such, or in which Being is forgotten in favour of being ordered in a system of causes and effects, of fully unfolded and enunciated reasons. When the forgetting of Being is complete and total, metaphysics is at once finished and totally realized in its deepest tendency. In fact, this total forgetting of Being is the total technical organization of a world in which there is no longer anything 'unforeseen' or historically new, nor anything that escapes the programmed concatenation of causes and effects. In the end of metaphysics as technology, the nexus between metaphysics, domination and will, which had hitherto remained hidden, becomes explicit. The system of total concatenation of causes and effects, prefigured by metaphysics in its 'vision' of the world and actualized by technology, is the expression of a will to dominate. Hence the Nietzschean will to power is simply the most coherent culmination of the history of Western metaphysics.

A number of contemporary Italian scholars, among them Massimo Cacciari, have pursued this Heideggerian interpretation of the history of metaphysics and the philosophy of Nietzsche, and have stressed the connection between 'negative thought' and 'rationalization', attempting to redeem Nietzsche and other avant-garde thinkers from the old reproach of Lukács, who assigned Nietzsche to the category of irrationalism. Negative thought, particularly in the form of the extreme voluntarism that emerges with Nietzsche, rather represents the furthest reach of authentic modern rationalism, a rationalism that elevates reason and its technical unfolding to a position of supremacy, free from all metaphysical or humanistic qualms, from all dependence vis-à-vis allegedly natural structures, laws of Being, things in themselves, and so on. From this point of view Nietzsche is as much the height of rationalism as is the pure conventionalism of science and the 'immanent' development of technology.

Despite its not always explicit polemic with Lukács, this interpretation seems to take a stand towards Heidegger's view of Nietzsche which is analogous to that of Lukács toward the Nazi Nietzsche of Baeumler. As far as Lukács was concerned, Baeumler had in fact been substantially correct in his interpretation of Nietzsche, and all that was needed was to 'change the slant' of his assessment. Similarly, the upholders of a 'rationalist' Nietzsche also regard Heidegger's interpretation of him as substantially beyond dispute: but in their approach to Nietzsche's technicist rationalism there is no hint of lamentation about the forgetting of Being, nor is there any anticipation of a possible new coming of Being. Instead they abandon all humanistic nostalgia and see Nietzsche simply as the most coherent expression of a situation that is outside our control, a situation that is nothing less than a Western destiny. If there is any liberation from alienation, it must lie at the end of a journey through the desert of the death of every humanistic illusion, through a totally administered world, through the unfolding of the will to power as technocracy. Unlike Lukács, Nietzsche here looks less like the symptom of a malady than the expression of a universal condition. Indeed, it is hard to see how this technicist interpretation of the will to power by scholars on the Left goes any further than merely affirming and accepting that same universal technicization or 'total organization' of the world. For such commentators Nietzsche is no longer a symptom, as he was for Lukács, but he is not a therapy either. The only cure is that of resolutely abandoning all illusion and facing up to the fact of the world as a totally administered system.

In all fairness, it is far from clear that Heidegger's view of Nietzsche is really beyond dispute. Its chief weakness is that it smacks of all the ontological and ultimately still metaphysical pathos to be found in Heidegger himself, and is thus difficult to sustain except within the confines of Heidegger's own ontological perspective. This raises the problem of how far it is possible to extrapolate Heidegger's interpretation of Nietzsche from the rest of his philosophy, but it is a point I do not wish to pursue here. As to the question of whether we should accept Heidegger's particular reading of the will to power, it must be said that there are serious difficulties. They can be neatly summed up in the title of this essay, which represents one of the titles to be found among Nietzsche's plans for the arrangement of the materials from his last years that were published posthumously. My thesis is that neither Heidegger (for systematic reasons connected with his entire interpretation of metaphysics) nor even his left-wing followers seem to have paid sufficient attention to the aesthetic model which in reality underlies the will to power, and which prevents us from identifying it *tout court* with the will to a total technocratic organization of the world.

The art/science polarity is a constant in Nietzsche's thought. Possibly its most significant moment comes in the fourth part of *Human, all too Human*, devoted to the study 'of the souls of artists and writers'. Of course, the idea of the will to power does not yet appear in this work, a work that is emblematic of what some see as Nietzsche's 'Enlightenment' period, when he tended to show a preference for 'scientific devotion to the true in any form, however plainly this may appear'[1] viewing art as *passé*, a relic of earlier and less mature epochs of the history of the human spirit. None the less, the work still provides the best starting-point, since in the period that begins with *Zarathustra* the terms of the opposition, and in particular the features attributed to art, remain substantially the same, except that art no longer appears to be a fact of the past and becomes one of the models, indeed the model, for what might rather unsatisfactorily be called the 'definition' of the will to power. But if art can fulfil this role of model, it is not by virtue of any arbitrary decision of Nietzsche's, attributable to some kind of 'aestheticism' on his part; rather it arises from a realization he came to while labouring to unmask morality and metaphysics during his 'middle' period (which begins with *Human, all too Human* and runs through *The Gay Science*) to the effect that art is pre-eminently the 'place' where, in the history of Western culture, there persists a dionysiac residuum, a form of liberty of the spirit, in other words, what in his last years he called the will to power.

This 'revaluation' of art is however something that comes to maturity in Nietzsche hand in hand with the maturation of his genealogical thought, summed up in aphorism 44 of *Daybreak*, where he claims that the more we know of origins the more insignificant they become. But in *Human, all too Human* Nietzsche is still in a sense at the beginning of this itinerary. He is still defining art as a form of the spirit that moves in the world of pure appearance, in contrast with science, which pursues and obtains truth. In aphorism 146, which more or less marks the beginning of the fourth part of *Human, all too Human*, a part which is in fact dedicated to artists and writers, the artist appears as one who has a weaker morality than the thinker in respect of truth. The artist is anxious to preserve the presuppositions that are most crucial for his art, namely, 'the fantastic, mythical, uncertain, extreme, the sense for the symbolical . . .' In a series of aphorisms Nietzsche alleges that these premisses are features of epochs coinciding with humanity's childhood. In these epochs the fantastic, the mythical and the symbolic are triumphs in the *investments* of factual reality by the imagination, fantasies and anthropomorphism, and this investment of the external, of the 'given' as we might put it, by the imagination, results from the pressure of the emotions, especially in that poetry's lightness and frivolity give temporary relief to the excessively passionate soul (HATH no. 154). This is in line with Nietzsche's view of tragedy, where the Apollonian vision is primarily a way of assuaging the force of the Dionysiac impulse. And yet the connection between art and emotion goes beyond this 'cathartic' function: for the artist, precisely to the extent that he is psychologically a child and anthropologically a kind of left-over of epochs in which the fantastic and the mythical predominated, also lives his passions and emotions in the manner appropriate to children and primitives, i.e. violently and impulsively (HATH no. 159). The phenomenon of inspiration itself is linked to these emotional mechanisms of art, for it is nothing but creative force (equivalent to the power that images, symbols, etc. have to invest the 'real') that has been subject to blockage at some point and overflows unexpectedly (HATH no. 156). The way the artist lives his own emotions so impetuously is simply the sign of the *excess* manifested by art in these pages of *Human, all too Human*; this excess lies both in the impetuosity of passion and, more fundamentally and constitutively, in the way the external is invested by the internal with its images, fantasies, symbols, etc.

Without forcing the texts, we may legitimately see two other features of art as linked to the idea of exceeding, its being surplus and its being the exception. Art is surplus precisely in its form of excess. Aphorism 154 cited above speaks of the way the Greeks managed to counterbalance the overly passionate soul by inventing fables that served to cover up, travesty and transfigure reality. However, this impulse to devise masks tends to become independent of its primordial function, namely, reintroducing equilibrium into the passions: it turns into a quite autonomous habit of lying. Art is equally surplus in respect of other spiritual forms, such as religion, morals and metaphysics, which Nietzsche views as things of the past. While the concluding aphorisms of the fourth part of *Human, all too Human* speak of 'feasts of memory' which now commemorate art, they also say that 'what is best in us has perhaps been inherited from feelings of past epochs'. In particular there is aphorism 213, 'wherever there is happiness, there is pleasure in absurdity', namely, the pleasure produced by art (in this case the comic) as it reverses the laws that prevail in the world of everyday 'reality'. None of the forms of the moral/metaphysical past of humanity 'unmasked' by Nietzsche in his 'Enlightenment' works has such an ambiguous and equivocal position as art. Art is a past, to be sure, but it is also a future, if we take seriously the assertion that there is no such thing as happiness without the pleasure of nonsense, i.e. without artistic travesty, invention and mask. In this sense, art *exceeds*[2] the decline which is the destiny of the forms of metaphysical 'lying', and it does so precisely to the extent that it differs from them in being play and exception. Thus aphorism 213 concludes by recalling the joy of the slave in the Saturnalia – the provisional suspension during feasts of the order of the social hierarchy and in general of the principle of reality.[3]

It is not my intention here to explore this connection between excess, surplus and exception. I want to make only one point about the last of these three terms. Exception might look like a sign of the weakness or 'unreality' of art (the 'Sunday of life', to use the Hegelian terminology, a merely temporary suspension of the laws of the real and of the hierarchical order of society). But this is not in fact the case if, as Nietzsche suggests, in the course of the exposition of his genealogical thought, that 'reality' too is actually at bottom nothing more than fable. For, in taking to the limit his enterprise of unmasking morals/metaphysics, Nietzsche ends up by unmasking 'belief in truth as the highest value', belief in 'real truth' as a norm terroristically working against appearance, fable, and hence also aesthetic experience. The result is to change the value and meaning of those character-istics of surplus/excess/exception inherent in art according to *Human, all too Human*, where they are ways of isolating art from that 'seriousness' which makes only scientific knowledge of the truth valid. This revaluation becomes evident in Nietzsche's transition from his second to his third period, in the discovery of the idea of eternal recurrence. The majority of the features of art he singled out in *Human, all too Human* still remain, but they cease to be a sign of regression (at least in the derogatory sense of the word); rather they become positive connotations of that exemplary form of excess which is art and which will unfold most completely in the idea of the will to power.

According to the hypothesis I want tentatively to sketch out here, to underline the significance of the will to power as art means to focus on the essentially destructuring aspect of the will to power. This runs counter to Heideggerian interpretations, which understand the will to power as the extreme unfolding of the rational and technical organization of the real by man, who has himself in turn also become an object of total planning. Here too one must try to understand the relation between Nietzsche and twentieth-century avant-garde literature and art, which certainly felt his influence and 'translated' it into creative terms.

The essentially destructuring significance of the will to power is at its most evident in those aspects of art that I have summed up by the idea of excess, aspects that are outlined in exemplary fashion in the fourth part of *Human, all too Human*. There art is, as we have seen, all that activity which involves the investing of the external by the internal, the imposition on 'things' of images, fantasies, symbolic values and so on, invented by the subject under the pressure of emotions and instinctual impulses. In *Human, all too Human* this activity still seems to be relegated to the category of things that have been made obsolete by the development of scientific man; and yet even in this work there are already hints that art is more than a mere relic of the past. Subsequently Nietzsche's thought moves towards a position summed up in the words of the title of a chapter in *Twilight of the Idols*: 'How the "Real World" at last became a myth'. There are no 'facts', there are only interpretations. There are only fables, and the fables are symbolic productions resulting from certain hierarchies of propulsive forces, giving rise to determinate configurations; for example, a certain interpretation 'prevails' as 'true' and becomes the norm, but it is actually a matter of force. What Nietzsche calls the world as will to power is this play of 'interpretations' imposing themselves without any 'facts', symbolic configurations arising from the play of forces and themselves becoming agents of the establishment of configurations of forces. This world is like a 'work of art that creates itself'.

How does 'destructuring' fit in with the will to power conceived in terms of this artistic mode? The key to this may also be found in the fragments of Nietzsche's last years, where art as a model for the will to power is not described so much in terms of 'grand style' or closed 'form' as it often seems, but in the terms of *Human, all too Human* – impetuosity of the passions. In fact here these passions become specifically the sexual instinct, the taste for lying, the arrogance of the artist in wanting to be thought a 'genius' and the imposition on things of configurations produced by the subject and yet almost entirely devoid of classic 'form'. Zarathustra's dance, an image so often present in the later Nietzsche, is not primarily an Apollonian fact (involving accomplished form, purity and transparence, stability, order and symmetry) but chaos and Dionysiac frenzy, tempered only by irony (which itself seems to have nothing Apollonian about it).

These models of a Nietzschean view of art, both in the period of *Human, all too Human* and after *Zarathustra*, ought to put us on guard against the mistake of thinking that will to power means primarily will to form, to definiteness and therefore always to domination. The will to power appears in its destructuring nature when it is seen as art and therefore as a production of symbols, which do not function solely or even mainly as 'equilibrators' of the passions, but rather as pulsive mechanisms themselves, not assuaging but activating the affective life. This emerges in a long fragment from the summer of 1887, labelled 'On European nihilism',[4] where, above all in paragraph nine, the discovery that there are no eternal values, stable natural structures or definitive sanctions guaranteed by God, but only conflicting forces, produces a movement in which the 'failures' perish; for if they shed all illusion and face up to the battle they are in, they either escape from their subjection to the powerful through a victorious struggle, or else they fall into such a state of neurosis that they constrain the powerful to exterminate them.

Nihilism, the discovery of the 'lie', the discovery that alleged 'values' and metaphysical structures are just a play of forces, is the revelation of the will to power as that which dislocates and subverts prevailing hierarchical relations. How it does this is precisely by unveiling them as relations of force rather than orders corresponding to 'values'. No one remains in the same position in the social hierarchy once the discovery has been made that values are nothing but positions of the will to power, whether of the strong or the weak (for the weak find in their own moral values a way of maintaining a sense of superiority *vis-à-vis* their oppressors in spite of their subjection). Nor does the internal hierarchy of individual subjects remain intact, for they discover even within themselves no pure recognition of values, but forces locked in combat and perpetually provisional systematizations. 'It is the value of such a crisis,' writes Nietzsche in the fragment referred to, alluding to the crisis of nihilism, 'that it purifies . . .' Of relevance here is the fact that in the writings of his last years Nietzsche very frequently lays stress on the 'selectivity' of the idea of eternal recurrence. In the light of the above fragment on nihilism, this selectivity can no longer be viewed simplistically merely as some ability to distinguish between those who are capable of enduring eternal recurrence and those who are not. Nietzsche certainly does think in such terms, but there is something more complex at the bottom of it all, something very clearly expressed in aphorism 341 of *The Gay Science*, on 'the greatest weight'.[5] One way of putting its conclusion might be this: 'How happy you must be to will the eternal recurrence of the moment.' This is in marked contrast to the stoic/ascetic position, i.e. 'How "strong" you have to be to accept the eternity of the moment you are living, in spite of everything.' Nietzsche's position corresponds with the doctrine of the will to power and the superman. Aphorism 341 also suggests that the meaning of the selectivity of eternal recurrence lies wholly in the conditions of its possibility 'How happy you must be' also means 'but actually how unhappy you are, how intolerable your situation is.' This is the same as the fragment on European nihilism, which speaks of the subversive effect produced in the weak and powerful alike by the discovery of the reality of power relations. It is a thesis that calls for an analytic comparison with the Hegelian dialectic of slave and master. There we see a coming to awareness that involves a merely temporary role reversal without any change in the essential nature of mastery and slavery; all that truly changes is the identity of master and slave. But in Nietzsche, selectivity means a primarily internal revolution within the subjects having this experience. 'How happy you must be to will eternal recurrence . . .' and therefore 'all that you are and all that you live is called into question, suspended in its claim to "validity" to peremptory reality.' We are not talking here about a change of places on the social ladder where, in a move that happens within the framework of the established hierarchy, we also preserve all of our internal hierarchies. If anything, this would occur if one interpreted the will to power in the technocratic Heideggerian manner. Such a will is no more than the will of the metaphysical or Christian/bourgeois subject of tradition, unfolding more completely and assuming dominion over the world. However, the texts in which Nietzsche denies that the will to power is will in the psychological sense of the term are not solely directed against the mistake that reads Schopenhauer's doctrine into his; they are also directed against all possible identification of the will to power with the will of metaphysical man, the free responsible technical organizer of the objective world. In that sort of conception of will there would be no room left for art, and hence there could be no explanation of why Nietzsche lays such persistent stress in his notes on the will to power as art.

Thus eternal recurrence and the will to power function mainly as a principle for destructuring actually reigning hierarchies, whether internal or external to the subject. This is demonstrated most clearly in Nietzsche's insistence on their selective character, as in aphorism 341 of The Gay Science. Neither of these theories has a 'positive' meaning capable of definitive formulation. Eternal recurrence does not primarily amount to saying *there is no* linear time but *there is* universal circularity. Equally, the will to power does not amount to saying that, in reality, *there are no* values, orders, etc . . ., but *there are* only forces. For these are metaphysical/descriptive readings of Nietzschean doctrines that fail to take note of the essentially antimetaphysical significance Nietzsche explicitly attributes to them.

It is particularly as the locus of destructuring activity that art constitutes the model Nietzsche has in mind when he talks about the will to power. I said earlier that the 'destructuring' features of art are already outlined in *Human, all too Human*. Now I want to show conclusively (though still only in outline) how these features are further clarified and developed in some of the posthumous fragments that Nietzsche had originally intended to bring together under the title of *The Will to Power*.

In these posthumous fragments the whole destructuring tendency of art is focused on its role as the *invigorator* of the emotions. In fact Zeitler talked as long ago as 1900 in his book on Nietzsche's aesthetics of a 'physiological aesthetic', referring to the writings of this final period. He was alluding precisely to that aspect of art which Nietzsche, even on the basis of positivistic readings, tends to interpret in a clearly materialistic fashion. I will recall only two long fragments, both from the spring of 1888:

Fragment 800. The counter-movement: *art*. The feeling of intoxication, in fact corresponding to an increase in strength; strongest in the mating season: new organs, new accomplishments, colours, forms; "becoming more beautiful" is a consequence of *enhanced* strength. Becoming more beautiful as the expression of a *victorious* will, of increased co-ordination, of a harmonizing of all the strong desires, of an infallibly perpendicular stress. Logical and geometrical simplification is a consequence of enhancement of strength:

conversely the apprehension of such a simplification again enhances the feeling of strength – High point of the development: the grand style.

Ugliness signifies the decadence of a type, contradiction and lack of co-ordination among the inner desires – signifies a decline in organizing strength, in "will", to speak psychologically.

The condition of pleasure called intoxication is precisely an exalted feeling of *power* – The sensations of space and time are altered: tremendous distances are surveyed and, as it were, for the first time apprehended; the extension of vision over greater masses and expanses; the refinement of the organs for the apprehension of much that is extremely small and fleeting; *divination*, the power of understanding with only the least assistance, at the slightest suggestion: "intelligent" *sensuality* – ; strength as a feeling of dominion in the muscles, as suppleness and pleasure in movement, as dance, as levity and *presto*; strength as pleasure in the proof of strength, as bravado, adventure, fearlessness, indifference to life or death – All these climactic moments of life mutually stimulate one another; the world of images and ideas of the one suffices as a suggestion for the others: – in this way, states finally merge into one another though they might perhaps have good reason to remain apart. For example: the feeling of religious intoxication and sexual excitation (– two profound feelings, co-ordinated to an almost amazing degree. What pleases all pious women, old or young? Answer: a saint with beautiful legs, still young, still an idiot). Cruelty in tragedy and sympathy (– also normally co-ordinated –) Spring, dance, music: – all competitions between the sexes – and even that Faustian "infinity in the breast."

Artists, if they are any good, are (physically as well) strong, full of surplus energy, powerful animals, sensual; without a certain overheating of the sexual system, a Raphael is unthinkable – Making music is another way of making children; chastity is merely the economy of an artist – and in any event, even with artists fruitfulness ceases when potency ceases – Artists should see nothing as it is, but fuller, simpler, stronger: to that end, their lives must contain a kind of youth and spring, a kind of habitual intoxication.[6]

Fragment 821. The countermovement of *art.*
Pessimism in art?
The artist gradually comes to love for their own sake the means that reveal a condition of intoxication: extreme subtlety and splendour of colour, definiteness of line, nuances of tone: and the *distinct* where otherwise, under normal conditions, distinctness is lacking. All distinct things, all nuances, to the extent that they recall these extreme enhancements of strength that intoxication produces, awaken this feeling of intoxication by association: the effect of works of art is to *excite the state that creates art* – intoxication.

What is essential in art remains its perfection of existence, its production of perfection and plenitude; art is essentially *affirmation, blessing, deification of existence* – What does a *pessimistic art* signify? Is it not a *contradictio?* – Yes. – Schopenhauer is *wrong* when he says that certain works of art serve pessimism. Tragedy does *not* teach "resignation" – To represent terrible and questionable things is in itself an instinct for power and magnificence in an artist: he does not fear them – There is no such thing as pessimistic art – Art affirms. Job affirms. – But Zola? But the Goncourts? – The things they display are ugly: but *that* they display them comes from their *pleasure in the ugly* – It's no good! If you think otherwise, you're deceiving yourselves. – How liberating is Dostoevsky![7]

The points I want to stress here are these: to begin with, the explicit link between beauty and the sexual impulse; then, in the first text, the idea of beautification as the 'expression of a victorious will . . . harmonization, logical and geometrical simplification . . . the grand style'. At this point the impulse/beauty/force connection would seem to resolve itself into an accomplished form, a form that has to do with force insofar as it is the expression of a victory. The relation between *form* and *force* indicated here seems to me to be another of the central themes or motifs in the aesthetic of the mature Nietzsche; it also seems to be crucial to the connection between art and the will to power. In the first part of fragment 821 this connection seems to resolve itself in the manner I have indicated, such that form is the result of the victory of a force that orders, subjects, simplifies and harmonizes; but the relationship takes on a different appearance at other points in these same texts. In the succeeding lines of the fragment the discourse moves on to inebriation, which involves a heightened sensibility, a propensity for dance, a linking up of worlds of images which stimulate and incite each other in turn to indefinite development. Art seems to become a place where religious rapture coincides with sexual excitation, while artists are revealed as endowed with exuberance, animal energy and sensuality. In both fragments 800 and 821 the feeling for nuances and the capacity to recognize and appreciate solidity of line, and hence perhaps form, are thus dependent on the state of overexcitation, exuberance or inebriation, i.e. on something that is not primarily an impulse to form, but which rather stands on the side of the Dionysiac negation of form. On one hand the power achieved by art seems to be related to its representation of the triumph of unitary organization over centrifugal thrust, multiplicity, mobility and the disorder of the impulses. On the other hand, it seems that the more Nietzsche strives to analyse the meaning of this victory of force in art, the more he realizes that the idea of the organic, of geometrical simplicity, of structural rigour crumbles in his hands. Art comes to look more and more like an activation of impulses recalcitrant to unification and coordination, forces so highly refined as to be almost pathological. Thus in fragments 800 and 821 the invigorating function of art is not exercised in the (artist's) domination of materials and tools or in the (spectator's) domination of passions, but rather in the potentiation of the passions as a means by which humans can assert themselves over and against the apparent negativity of existence.

On one hand, then, Nietzsche puts forward this conception of art as a pulsive mechanism with a destructuring effect insofar as it triggers the subject's impulses and so breaks up the subject's established hierarchies, stability and 'continuity' (which is what Plato was defending when he condemned dramatic poetry). By contrast, however, there is also Nietzsche's polemic, particularly in his final period, against 'decadent' art, *romantisme*, art which has forgotten the 'grand style' and has been reduced to an opiate, a mere stimulant for the emotions. As is well known, here also lies the root of his opposition to Wagner. Nevertheless I do not believe that the position of the later Nietzsche on art and literature can simply be reduced to a polarity between a kind of 'classicism' (the notion of 'grand style') and the decadent and emotionalistic features of the Romantic art of his day. Consider fragments 809, 812, 843, and 811 from the spring of 1888:

Fragment 809. All art exercises the power of suggestion over the muscles and senses, which in the artistic temperament are originally active: it always speaks only to artists – it speaks to this kind of a subtle flexibility of the body. The concept "layman" is an error. The deaf man is not a species of the man with good hearing.

All art works tonically, increases strength, inflames desire (i.e. the feeling of strength), excites all the more subtle recollections of intoxication – there is a special memory that penetrates such states: a distant and transitory world of sensations here comes back.

The ugly, i.e., the contradiction to art, that which is excluded from art, its No – every time decline, impoverishment of life, impotence, disintegration, degeneration are suggested even faintly, the aesthetic man reacts with his No. The effect of the ugly is depressing: it is the expression of a depression. It takes away strength, it impoverishes, it weighs down.

The ugly suggests ugly things; one can use one's states of health to test how variously an indisposition increases the capacity for imagining ugly things. The selection of things, interests, and questions changes. A state closely related to the ugly is encountered in logic, too: heaviness, dimness. Mecha-

100

nically speaking, equilibrium is lacking: the ugly limps, the ugly stumbles: antithesis to the divine frivolity of the dancer.

The aesthetic state possesses a superabundance of means of communication, together with an extreme receptivity for stimuli and signs. It constitutes the high point of communication and transmission between living creatures – it is the source of languages. This is where languages originate: the languages of tone as well as the languages of gestures and glances. The more complete phenomenon is always the beginning: our faculties are subtilized out of more complete faculties. But even today one still hears with one's muscles, one even reads with one's muscles.

Every mature art has a host of conventions as its basis – in so far as it is a language. Convention is the condition of great art, *not* an obstacle-

Every enhancement of life enhances man's power of communication, as well as his power of understanding. Empathy with the souls of others is originally nothing moral, but a physiological susceptibility to suggestion: "sympathy", or what is called "altruism," is merely a product of that psychomotor rapport which is reckoned a part of spirituality (*induction psycho-motrice*, Charles Féré thinks). One never communicates thoughts: one communicates movements, mimic signs, which we then trace back to thoughts.[8]

Fragment 812. I set down here a list of psychological states as signs of a full and flourishing life that one is accustomed today to condemn as morbid. For by now we have learned better than to speak of healthy and sick as of an antithesis: it is a question of degrees. My claim in this matter is that what is today called "healthy" represents a lower level than that which under favorable circumstances *would be* healthy – that we are relatively sick –

The artist belongs to a still stronger race. What would be harmful and morbid in us, in him is nature – But one objects to us that it is precisely the impoverishment of the machine that makes possible extravagant powers of understanding of every kind of suggestion: witness our hysterical females.

An excess of sap and force can bring with it symptoms of partial constraint, of sense hallucinations, susceptibility to suggestion, just as well as can impoverishment of life: the stimulus is differently conditioned, the effect remains the same – But the after-effect is not the same; the extreme exhaustion of all morbid natures after their nervous eccentricities has nothing in common with the states of the artist, who does not have to atone for his good periods – He is rich enough for them: he is able to squander without becoming poor.

As one may today consider "genius" as a form of neurosis, so perhaps also the artistic power of suggestion – and indeed our *artists* are painfully like hysterical females!!! But that is an objection to "today," not to "artists."

Inartistic states: those of objectivity, mirroring, suspended will – (*Schopenhauer's* scandalous misunderstanding when he took art for a bridge to the denial of life) – Inartistic states: among those who become impoverished, withdraw, grow pale, under whose eyes life suffers: – the Christian.[9]

Fragment 843. Romanticism: an ambiguous question, like everything modern.[10]

Fragment 811. Countermovement: *art.*

It is exceptional states that condition the artist – all of them profoundly related to and interlaced with morbid phenomena – so it seems impossible to be an artist and not to be sick.

Physiological states that are in the artist as it were molded into a "personality" and that characterize men in general to some degree:

1. *intoxication*: the feeling of enhanced power; the inner need to make of things a reflex of one's own fullness and perfection;

2. the *extreme sharpness* of certain senses, so they understand a quite different sign language – and create one – the condition that seems to be a part of many nervous disorders – ; extreme mobility that turns into an extreme urge

102

to communicate; the desire to speak on the part of everything that knows how to make signs – ; a need to get rid of oneself, as it were, through signs and gestures; ability to speak of oneself through a hundred speech media – an *explosive* condition. One must first think of this condition as a compulsion and urge to get rid of the exuberance of inner tension through muscular activity and movements of all kinds; then as an involuntary co-ordination between this movement and the processes within (images, thoughts, desires) – as a kind of automatism of the whole muscular system impelled by strong stimuli from within – ; inability to prevent reaction; the system of inhibitions suspended, as it were. Every inner movement (feeling, thought, affect) is accompanied by vascular changes and consequently by changes in color, temperature, and secretion. The suggestive power of music, its "*suggestion mentale*"; –

3. the *compulsion to imitate*: an extreme irritability through which a given example becomes contagious – a state is divined on the basis of signs and immediately enacted – An image, rising up within, immediately turns into a movement of the limbs – a certain suspension of the will – (Schopenhauer!!!) A kind of deafness and blindness towards the external world – the realm of admitted stimuli is sharply defined.

This is what distinguishes the artist from laymen (those susceptible to art): the latter reach the high point of their susceptibility when they receive; the former as they give – so that an antagonism between these two gifts is not only natural but desirable. The perspectives of these two states are opposite: to demand of the artist that he should practice the perspective of the audience (of the critic –) means to demand that he should impoverish himself and his creative power – It is the same here as with the difference between the sexes: one ought not to demand of the artist, who gives, that he should become a woman – that he should receive.

Our aesthetics hitherto has been a woman's aesthetics to the extent that only the receivers of art have formulated their experience of "what is beautiful?" In all philosophy hitherto the artist is lacking –

This, as the foregoing indicates, is a necessary mistake; for the artist who began to understand himself would misunderstand himself: he ought not to look back, he ought not to look at all, he ought to give.

It is to the honor of an artist if he is unable to be a critic – otherwise he is half and half, he is "modern."[11]

These passages provide interesting confirmation of the de-structuring effect aesthetic experience has on the subject; according to the first of the above fragments, art imparts mobility to the body (one feels and reads, for instance, with the muscles). But the most important thing here is to see how in both texts 'morbid' states appear to be indispensable and positive elements of artistic being. The artist is in an 'explosive' condition and 'it seems impossible to be an artist and not to be able to be sick.' What is at work here is not Schopenhauer's relating of genius to madness; for Nietzsche there is no 'pure' vision of ideas. In fact the morbidity of artistic states has exactly the opposite meaning to what it has for Schopenhauer, where it is linked to a fundamentally ascetic viewpoint. Nietzsche's 'morbidity' activates the emotions, it makes us live 'other lives', it intensifies the dynamic of the impulses and thus unbalances the whole hierarchy according to which the subject is structured. The allusion to the 'person' in fragment 811 should be read in this sense.

Although I cannot linger on them here, there are various texts in which Nietzsche clearly distinguishes between a degenerate art and an affirmative art, basing himself, for example, on the fact that the former presents itself as a surrogate for passions that are not truly lived but only imagined. It does not seem legitimate to interpret these in a way that would sustain a 'classicist' reading of the later Nietzschean aesthetic. Nietzsche's polemic is directed against *romantisme* not so much for its dissolution of form as for the moralism that always accompanies romantic sentimentalism. On this point it is worth citing a fragment from the autumn of 1887:

Fragment 823. The moralization of the arts – Art as freedom from moral narrowness and corner-perspectives; or as mockery of them. Flight into nature, where its beauty is coupled with frightfulness. Conception of the great human being.

– Fragile, useless luxury souls, troubled even by a breath, "beautiful souls."

– To awaken deceased ideals in all their merciless severity and brutality, as the most magnificent monsters they are.

– A joyful delight in the psychological insight into the sinuosity and unconscious play-acting of all moralized artists.

– The falsity of art – to bring to light its immorality.

– To bring to light "basic idealizing powers" (sensuality, intoxication, superabundant animality).[12]

Clearly, the 'idealizing powers' Nietzsche talks about at the end of the passage, namely the 'sensuality, intoxication, superabundant animality', function as such only if the 'idealization' is understood not as the imposition of a rounded and perfected form, but rather as an overflowing of the internal onto the external, something which in the same fragment is called the 'falsity' of art. To assert such an idealization is also to indicate a relation between *force* and *form* different from the one that other texts of Nietzsche's have, with some justification, led commentators to view as characteristic of the Nietzschean aesthetic. Force does not resolve itself into the imposition of a form; rather, these texts I have been referring to suggest that form is for ever being exploded by a play of forces, of particular forces, namely the body's instincts, sensuality and animal vitality. In this sense art functions as the place where the will to power and the Dionysiac are unfolded. It also functions in general as the model of a will to power that is in no way identifiable with the technocratic *ratio* of a totally organized world. On the contrary, force operates against form inasmuch as it reveals and throws into crisis the violence of form, just as the will to power acts as an unmasking and destructuring agent in the face of all allegedly 'natural', eternal, divine and objective orders. The 'grand style' is in no sense the only possible destiny of true art. On the contrary, today it no longer seems even possible or desirable, at least for music, which was in Nietzsche's eyes the art *par excellence*. On this it is worth reading fragment 842 from the spring of 1888:

Fragment 842. "Music" – and the grand style. – The greatness of an artist cannot be measured by the "beautiful feelings" he arouses: leave that idea to females. But according to the degree to which he approaches the grand style, to which he is capable of the grand style. This style has this in common with great passion, that it disdains to please; that it forgets to persuade; that it commands; that it *wills* – To become master of the chaos one is; to compel one's chaos to become form: to become logical, simple, unambiguous, mathematics, *law* – that is the grand ambition here. – It repels; such men of force are no longer loved – a desert spreads around them, a silence, a fear as in the presence of some great sacrilege – All the arts know such aspirants to the grand style: why are they lacking in music? No musician has yet built as that architect did who created the Palazzo Pitti – Here lies a problem. Does music perhaps belong to that culture in which the domain of men of force of all kinds has ceased? Does the concept grand style ultimately stand in contradiction to the soul of music – to the "woman" in our music? –

I here touch upon a cardinal question: where does our entire music belong? The ages of classical taste knew nothing to compare with it: it began to blossom when the Renaissance world had attained its evening, when "freedom" had departed from morals and even from men: – is it part of its character to be counter-Renaissance? Is it the sister of the Baroque style, since it is in any case its contemporary? Is music, modern music, not already decadence? –

Once before I pointed to this question: whether our music is not a piece of counter-Renaissance in art? whether it is not next-of-kin to the Baroque style? whether it has not grown up in contradiction to all classical taste, so that all ambitions to become classical are forbidden to it by its nature?

The answer to this first-rank question of values would not remain in doubt if the proper inferences had been drawn from the fact that music achieved its greatest ripeness and fullness as romanticism – once again as a movement of reaction against classicism.

Mozart – a delicate and amorous soul, but entirely eighteenth century, even when he is serious. – Beethoven the first great romantic, in the sense of the *French* conception of romanticism, as Wagner is the last great romantic – both instinctive opponents of classical taste, of severe style – to say nothing of "grand" style.[13]

The tone of this text destroys any lingering suspicion that this 'surplus' of music, its being 'counter-Renaissance' and 'woman', might be viewed negatively by Nietzsche. On the contrary, he is putting forward the hypothesis that music henceforth belongs to a culture in which the fetishism of form and grand style is at an end, because the reign of the man of violence is at an end.

If we really take such texts seriously, it becomes impossible to identify the will to power with Western man's assumption of technocratic domination and the consequent liquidation of every metaphysical residue, through a total realization of metaphysics in the Heideggerian sense. Over against the neorationalistic interpretation of Nietzsche, these texts impose a reading that might legitimately be called 'radical hermeneutics'. The world of symbolic forms – philosophy, art, and cultural set – maintains autonomy *vis-à-vis* technological rationality; it is the place where the subject, to whom technique has given the capacity to exploit the world, actually ex-ploits, dis-locates, and destructures itself as subjected subject, as the last incarnation of the structures of domination. The Heideggerian hope of a new epoch of Being must probably pass (beyond the deployment of metaphysics in the complete organization of the world) through this operation of radically disorganizing the subject,[14] which for Nietzsche is accomplished first and foremost in the will to power as art.

Notes

1   *Human, all too Human*, no. 146.
2   Vattimo here plays on the common root of the Italian words
     eccesso (here translated as *excess*), *eccedenza* (here *surplus*) and
     eccezione (here *exception*). All are of course linked with the
     word *eccedere* (*exceed*). (Translator's note.)
3   For a treatment of this whole topic of art as a form of
     metaphysical culture which in many ways transcends the
     limits of that culture, keeping alive the embers of the
     Dionysiac and constituting the possible basis for its rebirth,
     see my *Il soggetto e la maschera. Nietzsche e il problema della
     liberazione*, Milan, 1979.
4   WP pp. 35–9.
5   *The greatest weight.* – What, if some day or night a
     demon were to steal after you into your loneliest loneli-
     ness and say to you: "This life as you now live it and
     have lived it, you will have to live once more and
     innumerable times more; and there will be nothing new
     in it, but every pain and every joy and every thought and
     sigh and everything unutterably small or great in your
     life will have to return to you, all in the same succession
     and sequence – even this spider and this moonlight
     between the trees, and even this moment and I myself.
     The eternal hourglass of existence is turned upside down
     again and again, and you with it, speck of dust!"
          Would you not throw yourself down and gnash your
     teeth and curse the demon who spoke thus? Or have you
     once experienced a tremendous moment when you
     would have answered him: "You are a god and never
     have I heard anything more divine." If this thought
     gained possession of you, it would change you as you
     are or perhaps crush you. The question in each and every
     thing, "Do you desire this once more and innumerable
     times more?" would lie upon your actions as the greatest
     weight. Or how well disposed would you have to
     become to yourself and to life *to crave nothing more
     fervently* than this ultimate eternal confirmation and seal?

108

(*The Gay Science*, trans. W. Kaufmann, New York, 1974, pp. 273–4).

6   WP no. 800, pp. 420–1.
7   WP no. 821, pp. 434–5.
8   WP no. 809, pp. 427–8.
9   WP no. 812, p. 430.
10 WP no. 843, p. 445.
11 WP no. 811, p. 428–9.
12 WP no. 823, p. 435.
13 WP no. 842, pp. 443–4.
14 Cf. the passage from 'The Age of the World Picture' quoted on p. 59.

5

An-Denken: *Thinking and the Foundation*

1 *Foundationless Thinking*

Heidegger writes in *On Time and Being* (1962)

> To think Being itself explicitly requires disregarding Being
> to the extent that it is only grounded and interpreted in terms
> of beings and for beings as their ground, as in all metaphy-
> sics. To think Being exactly requires us to relinquish Being as
> the ground of beings in favour of the giving which prevails
> concealed in unconcealment, that is, in favour of the *es gibt*
> (there is) (TB p. 6).

TEXTS like these, typical of the so-called 'late Heidegger',
seem to justify styling him the theorist of 'foundationless
thinking'. Further justification for this label may be found in
the fact that in Italy at least,[1] and to a lesser extent in France,[2]
the most recent wave of interest in Heidegger has brought
along with it an emphasis on the closeness of Heidegger to
Wittgenstein. These two are seen as responsible for the
definitive elimination of the very idea that philosophy might
have a foundation; hence also for the elimination of philosophy itself, in favour of a new thinking located in pure
groundlessness.

There is nothing revolutionary about discussing Heidegger in relation to Wittgenstein. Gadamer himself noted the analogy between his own ontological thinking on language, with its many links to Heidegger, and the Wittgensteinian idea of *Sprachspiele*. Karl Otto Apel's philosophy of communication is also based on the possibility of a meeting between existential/ontological thought (as represented by Heidegger) and analytical thought (especially Wittgenstein). In Apel the Heidegger–Wittgenstein connection takes the form of a recognition that in Wittgenstein too the ontological ramifications of language are definitively revealed. But when Heidegger is seen as a philosopher of foundationless thinking, it is this Wittgenstein dimension that weighs most heavily. In this perspective, to expound their affinity means to recognize how in Heidegger, in the epoch of accomplished metaphysics, or in the world of the total technical organization of beings, thinking has no other task than to devote itself entirely to the accomplishment of the technical domination of the world. The argument would be that ever since the emergence of metaphysics, thinking has always questioned beings as to their being, ever since Plato identifying *Seiendheit* with the presence of that which is present. In the age of accomplished metaphysics, thinking takes the final step along this way: it thinks Being in terms of being represented, a being represented that depends entirely on the re-presenting subject. Of course, 'represented' does not here mean 'imagined, fantasized, or dreamed up': it means 'brought to consist, to being' through rigorous procedures, the procedures of experimental science and the technology that both depends on science and founds it in its very possibility. If thinking in the age of metaphysics, and of philosophy as it has unfolded, has depended on such questioning of the being of beings, now that the essence of metaphysics has been made totally explicit by technology the question has lost all meaning. Thinking is changing its tone, it is being *be-stimmt* in a different way, the way that

111

Heidegger finds outlined in Nietzsche and in his notions of the eternal recurrence of the same, the will to power and the superman. From this point of view the dance and the laughter of Nietzsche's Zarathustra appear to be deeply serious activities. They only 'remain on the surface', but the surface itself is far from being accidental, committed to the movement of desire and 'irrational' vitality. For, as with the Wittgenstein of the *Investigations*, the game is a game only by virtue of the fact of its having *rules*. The legitimacy of these rules is not founded on anything other than the fact that they are given. There is no 'game of games', nor any fundamental ontology. We must forget about Being as foundation, remaining quite unnostalgically within the 'games' there are, taking on once and for all the task of promoting the multiple techniques of reason. The Heideggerian term 'destiny', which is central to this interpretation, points to the duty of Western man finally to assume conscious dominion over the earth. And yet, precisely insofar as it is a destiny, this dominion is denuded of all those aspects of arrogance and festive triumphalism that have traditionally accompanied dominion and power. The man of the will to power is no more than a *functionary* of the universal deployment of the technico-bureaucratic domination of the world.

2   The Withdrawal of Being: Calculation and Meditation

There is no sense in responding to such an interpretation by adducing a vague image of Heidegger as an opponent of science and technology, dreaming of an idyllic existence modelled on some imaginary Black Forest peasant or shepherd. Rather it is better to begin by recognizing that Heidegger's thinking about the possibility of going beyond metaphysics has its own particular complexity, one which may perhaps conceal the grounds for a more productive

approach to the discussion (and the refutation) of the interpretation I have just described. The essay on the *Ueberwindung der Metaphysik* is an excellent illustration of the complexity I am referring to. In the parallel between *Ueberwindung* and *Verwindung* there is a reminder of the fact that in
reality we can never overcome metaphysics, not simply in
the sense that it is not something that can be 'abolished like
an opinion' (EP p. 85) but also, more fundamentally, insofar
as 'metaphysics overcome in this way does not disappear. It
returns transformed, and remains in dominance as the continuing difference of Being and beings' (ibid.). There might
thus appear to be two ways of justifying the thesis according
to which Heidegger appeals to Western man to assume
absolute dominion over the earth, to discard all nostalgia and
live in the forgetfulness of Being. First, we might say that a
possible *Ueberwindung* of metaphysics can come about only
through a long *Verwindung* of metaphysics; that is to say, it
can be accomplished only as a final culmination of a process
that experiences metaphysics through to the end, thereby
totally and boldly accepting even the technical destiny of
modern man. Or in the second place we might say that on a
more radical level the *Ueberwindung–Verwindung* nexus may
be taken as an expression of the fact that we can never
overcome metaphysics, whether in this or in any other
possible epoch of Being. And this would seem to militate in
favour of the thesis that thinking's sole task today is to
identify with the destiny of the deployed domination of
technology; for only thus would thinking correspond to the
transmission (*Schickung*) of Being.

In Heidegger this *Schickung* seems to be inseparable from
the holding back of Being in the very moment when *Es gibt*,
in the moment when Being gives (itself), allowing beings to
appear. In its *Es gibt*, Being 'withdraws in favour of the gift
(*Gabe*) which it gives. That gift is thought and conceptua-
lized from then on exclusively as Being in relation to beings.
A giving which gives only its gift, but in the giving holds

itself back and withdraws, such a giving we call sending (*Schicken*)' (TB pp. 8–9). What constitutes the epochal character of Being is precisely this fact that Being holds back and withdraws even in the very moment that '*Es gibt*'. Epoch does not mean 'a span of time in occurrence, but rather the fundamental trait of sending, the actual holding-back of itself in favour of the discernibility of the gift, that is, of Being with regard to (*in Hinblick auf*) the grounding (*Ergründung*) of beings' (TB p. 9). To correspond to the *Gabe* of Being (which is always what it is in both senses of the genitive, neither of which may be thought as standing alone) cannot therefore mean to grasp the actual Being that gives. The thing that is perceived is always only the *Gabe*, the gift, never the offering and giving as such. The forgetting of Being that is characteristic of metaphysics and that corresponds to this 'fundamental trait' of *Schickung* cannot be understood in contrast to a 'remembering of Being' which would grasp it as present. Only a mistake like this can lead to a reading of Heidegger's philosophy as negative theology which, as theology, will always remain tied to the idea of a deployed presence, even if it is attainable only at the end of a long journey through regions of absence. The forgetfulness of Being in Heidegger never implies any possible condition (whether initial or final) of relatedness to Being as deployed presence.

However, the question is to discover and clarify the difference that subsists, in the context of the fundamental feature of *Schickung* (to the effect that every giving of Being involves its holding back and withdrawing), between a 'merely calculative' thought and a possible 'reflective thought' (SVG p. 199). Characterized though it be by the withholding of Being, not every *Schickung* involves a rigidification of the identification of Being with the presence of that which is present and the consequent culmination in the technical domination of the world. *Der Satz vom Grund* distinguishes between the call (*Anspruch*) of the principle of

114

reason, which dominates calculative thinking, and the *Zu-spruch*, the encouraging reminder, which speaks beyond and through this call (e.g. SVG p. 203). In *On Time and Being* there is another allusion to this possibility of a reflective or meditative thought as distinct from a merely calculative thought:

> But what gives us the right to characterize Being as presen-cing (*Anwesen*)? This question comes too late. For this character (*Prägung*) of Being has long since been decided without any contribution or merit of ours. Thus we are bound to the characterization of Being as presencing. It derives its binding force from the beginning of the uncon-cealment of Being as something that can be said, that is, can be thought. Ever since the beginning of Western thinking with the Greeks, all saying of 'Being' and 'is' has been held in remembrance of the mandatory definition of Being as pres-encing (*Anwesen*). This has been equally true for the thinking that directs the most modern technology and industry, *though by now only in a certain sense* (TB pp. 6–7).

I have italicized the last few words because I believe they pinpoint the difference between the withholding that is the fundamental feature of Being as *Schickung*, and the metaphy-sical rigidification of presence as it unfolds in the final technological domination of the world and in the reduction of Being to objectness. Doubtless it is a destiny of thinking as such (and the text cited speaks of thinkability in general) to be linked with a characterization of Being as presence; but this characterization must not necessarily nor always be identified with *Vorhandenheit* and *Zuhandenheit*, i.e. with the pure presence that dominates thinking which is modelled on science, or with the instrumentality to which our day-to-day dealings with being refer. Those two modes in which the Being of beings is given as analysed in *Being and Time* may legitimately be identified with the *objectness* discussed in the works that followed it (cf. PLT p. 167) for in the world of technology as accomplished metaphysics all *Vorhandenheit*, all presence-at-hand is reduced to a belonging to an 'equipment' (*Rüstung*), i.e. is reduced to an instrumentality albeit of an increasingly abstract type. What happens in metaphysics and then in its technical fruition, and what distinguishes metaphysics from the Greek *Frühe*, is precisely the reduction of *Anwesen* to objectness as the identity of *Vorhandenheit* and *Zuhandenheit*, an identity that is given in the reduction of everything to *Bestand*, to 'standing-reserve' (QT p. 17). The reduction of *Anwesen* to objectness excludes from presence the dimension of *Abwesen*, absence (TB p. 7). Above all it covers and forgets the nature of presence as *Anwesen-lassen* or *Schickung*: 'thought with regard to what presences, presencing shows itself as letting-presence . . . Letting-presence shows its character in bringing into unconcealment. To let presence means: to unconceal, to bring into openness. In unconcealing prevails a giving, the giving that gives presencing, that is, Being, in letting-presence' (TB p. 5).

What makes metaphysical thought 'fallen' is not the fact that Being is given to it as presence, but rather the rigidification of presence into objectness. We can welcome presence without rigidifying it into objectness, inasmuch as we recall presence in its nature as *Anwesen-lassen*, i.e. as the occurrence of unveiling or *a-létheia*. The crucial thing about preSocratic thinkers like Parmenides and Heraclitus is the fact that their poeticizing thought resounds with the call of presence as *Anwesen-lassen*, even though it is not thematized as such (e.g. TB p. 7). Those early thinkers responded to a call (*Geheiss*) of Being as *Lichtung*, 'but yet without naming it, or giving it thought, (*bedenken*) as such' (WT p. 168). The drift of this, and its numerous variants in Heidegger, is that at the dawn of Western thought presence is still announced as *Anwesen-lassen*; in the course of the history of metaphysics from Plato on, presence becomes rigidly identified with the pure being-present of what is present; no further attention is paid to the 'eventual' character of presence, until presence is in the end

116

totally reduced to objectness, to the *Bestand* of technology as accomplished metaphysics. If thinking wants to overcome metaphysics, it cannot try to escape from oblivion by grasping Being as something that is present, for in doing so it would become even more lost in the metaphysical 'erring' that forgets ontological difference. But can it try to relocate itself in the condition of the first thinkers, who did indeed respond to the *Geheiss* of Being as *Anwesenlassen*, but not in the manner that we must respond to it today? What makes us different from the early thinkers is the fact that there comes between us and them the deployment of the entire history of metaphysics, which is a destiny even in the sense that it substantially alters the way the question of Being can be formulated again today.

There must then be a mode of meditating Being which, without presenting it as something present, still manages to achieve that 'leap' out of science and philosophy discussed in *What is called Thinking?* (p. 41). As to how this leap is to be made, the 1962 lecture quoted at the beginning of this essay states that it must take leave of Being as foundation, indeed, 'forget it', in favour of a consideration of the giving that plays hidden in the unveiling occurrence of *Es gibt*. Does this paying no heed to Being as foundation point in the direction of 'a thinking without foundation'?

The difficulty here is that at the beginning we defined foundationless thinking as technical thinking, the thinking appropriate to the various technologies as games that cannot be unified in the perspective of fundamental ontology; and this thinking seems to be precisely the thinking that *Der Satz vom Grund* describes as calculative thinking, entirely subject to the call of the principle of reason, and therefore foundational thought *par excellence*. That which, on the basis of this and other Heideggerian texts, we might succeed in calling foundationless thinking, or better, thought that occurs outside the dominion of the principle of sufficient reason, has features that are completely opposed to the 'unfoundedness' of technical thinking, which unfolds as the organization of all beings in a system of 'founders' and 'foundeds', even if this system itself is founded on nothing. For technical thinking, and for what I have described as foundationless thinking, such a situation (of the ultimate unfoundedness of a world governed by the principle of reason) is an issue that does not merit any particular attention; and yet for Heidegger it is rather the *Denk-würdiges par excellence* (cf. SVG p. 210). But what would it mean to question such a state of affairs? Would it not be another questioning of it in order to call it back to some foundation? What does it mean to think?

'Science does not think', writes Heidegger (WT p. 134). He says this not because science lacks philosophy's ability to ground its own objects and discourse. Although philosophy certainly does perform such grounding we must learn to 'leap away' from it too, if we want to listen to the call of Being (cf. WT p. 41). In the epoch of metaphysics science belongs as much to foundational logic as philosophy does. The 'counting' and calculating of science is not mere enumeration; for science, counting means 'counting on', in other words being able to be sure about something, about an ever-increasing number of things. Science responds to the call of the principle of reason with a *Nach-stellen*, a pursuing and capturing, which is also a *Fest-stellen*, a making secure, a founding, a giving of stability (cf. QT p. 15 and note and *passim*). Science is thus animated by that 'spirit of revenge' from which Zarathustra wants to liberate man, the spirit that consists in lashing out against time and its 'it was'. Earlier than science, this spirit dominated and shaped the entirety of metaphysics. For this reason metaphysics, and then science, thought Being as absolute stability of presence, as eternity, that is as *independent of time* (WT p. 102). The final culmination of metaphysics consists in liberation from the spirit of revenge, which nevertheless merely brings to fuller accomplishment its revolt against time. This is the Nietzschean doctrine of the eternal recurrence of the same, which, as Nietzsche puts it, is 'the extremest approximation of a world of Becoming to the world of Being' (WT p. 108, with a reference to *The Will to Power*, no. 617). The Nietzschean eternal recurrence is not a 'theory'; it is the thinking appropriate to the world of modern technology, in which total planning seems to have excluded, or to be on the point of excluding, every '*es war*' (aside from death, of which I will speak later), giving shape to a world in which becoming is in fact taken to its point of greatest possible coincidence with Being as being-present.

The alternative to the thinking that subjects itself totally to the call of the *Satz vom Grund* is the thinking that is able to make the 'leap', the *Sprung* – but not into the void (even if it must be a leap towards the *Ab-grund*, or the absence of foundation: cf. SVG p. 186). The leap does not go into the void, instead it finds a *Boden*, a soil, indeed *the* soil 'upon which we live and die, if we are honest with ourselves' (WT p. 41). Does this too constitute the attainment of the kind of solidity that is sought by science with its *Fest-stellungen*? Even if the *Boden* is characterized by a stability that is surer and safer than that of the *Grund*, where does that get us? However, there is a difference between *Grund* and *Boden*, and it is described in *Der Satz vom Grund*, where Heidegger writes: 'the total predominance of the *Anspruch* to the *Zu-stellung* of the sufficient reason (*Grund*) threatens to strip man of all hope of belonging to a homeland and robs him of the *Grund* and soil (*Boden*) that offers him the possibility of rootedness' (SVG p. 60). Obviously he is not talking here about replacing the *Grund* with the 'patria', substituting the rootedness of an 'organic' community for membership in a society of free and equal citizens founded on explicit contract and stipulation; something very different is at stake. *Boden*, as soil or humus, recalls the idea of *Anwesen-lassen*; in suggesting a depth from which something can 'be born' (rather than causally derive) it names presence as *provenance*. It is like the term *a-létheia*, leading thought towards that way

119

of relating to Being which, without going beyond the 'fundamental feature' of *Schickung*, its epochality, does not in the least forget this epochality, but thinks of it as that which withholds and withdraws in the giving of the '*Es gibt*' itself.

3   *Andenken: Heidegger contra Schiller*

That thought which 'lets go of Being as foundation', leaping into the *Boden* and responding to the *Zuspruch* of presence as *Anwesenlassen*, is what Heidegger defines in terms of memory and recollection: *Denken* as *Gedächtnis, Denken* as *Andenken*. It is no accident that in the world of metaphysics technologically deployed, as described in Nietzsche's saying about the 'wasteland' that 'grows' (cf. WT p. 29) Mnemosyne no longer has rights of citizenship. 'Devastation is the high-velocity expulsion of Mnemosyne' (WT p. 30). The reason Heidegger talks about Mnemosyne is that, to illustrate his description of modern man as 'growing in the desert', he recalls some lines from one of Hölderlin's unfinished hymns, a hymn whose tentative list of possible titles included that of 'Mnemosyne':

> *Ein Zeichen sind wir, deutungslos*
> *Schmerzlos sind wir und haben fast*
> *Die Sprache in der Fremd verloren.* (WT p. 10)

These lines, with their reference to the 'sign that doesn't point to anything' and then to suffering, contain something of the global sense of what we find in the Heideggerian idea of *Andenken*.

What is the characteristic feature of thinking as *Andenken*? This thinking that lets go of Being as foundation and manages to think *Anwesen* as *Anwesenlassen*, manages to move towards thinking Being *properly* – why should it be

Andenken? Because memory is the way of thinking *Schik-kung*, the transmission or sending of Being as *sending*. In fact *Schickung* is such that, in the giving of the '*Es gibt*', giving itself withholds and withdraws in favour of the presence of the being that it lets be. Founding thought concentrates exclusively on the entity and on its Being as being present, without thinking it in its provenance. The way in which this thought relates to its object is as presencing (*Verge-genwärtigung*) or representation. Representation is the mode of being of thought in the epoch when Being is given as objectness. But the thought that, instead of thinking Being as the presence of what is present, strives to think presence in its provenance, cannot relate to this provenance by present-ing and re-presenting it. *Schickung* lets itself be thought only as always already having happened, as a gift from which the giving has always already withdrawn.

This is certainly what Heidegger is alluding to in the second section of *Identity and Difference*, when he says that for him, by contrast with Hegel, it is a question of thinking *difference as difference* (ID p. 47). Being can only be thought as difference, and therefore in a differing contrasted to the presence of the *objectum* of re-presentation. That thought which perpetually thinks its own object as deferred,[3] as constitutively not present, is *Gedächtnis*, *Andenken*, memory. It is true that even a computer has memory, is memory, but memory as that human faculty through which one can *erinnern* and *behalten* (WT p. 150). Memory understood as a faculty is still entirely caught up in the horizon of instru-mentality, of objectness and presence-at-hand. It is the mere capacity for presenting something that for the moment is not. The memory of the computer, then, corresponds strictly to the seizing and securing procedures of sciences, which, in the very act of ascertaining actually *block* the memory from rising above the *Grund* (the result is as it were to exorcize *Andenken* itself through its 'parody' in the procedure of founding).

Andenken 'is something other than the ephemeral making present of the past'.[4] Its relation to what it thinks about is closer to a *Verabschieden*, in one of the senses which that term has in German: seeing off that which has served its time, which has passed in accordance with its term, which has been accomplished (cf. WT p. 146). And Being as *Schik-kung* – which still resonates in essential words, as in the *Denken/Danken/Gedächtnis* nexus – is basically such that it cannot fail to remain in the unsaid and in the almost forgotten (cf. WT p. 153). We can never re-encapsulate it as such in language (ibid.).

This impotence of memory is expressed in the connection that lives on in language between *Denken/Gedächtnis* and *Danken*, or between thought/memory and thanking. Precisely to the extent that it is not reducible to the faculty of presenting that which is for the moment absent, memory is essentially an encounter between thinking and that which Dasein is and possesses as most proper to it and constitutive of it. Memory is 'the concentration of our disposition' as 'the gathering of the constant intention of everything that the heart holds in present being' (WT p. 141). In relation to this 'object' encountered by memory, thought takes shape as *Dank*, thanking; and this signifies above all that thought encounters this 'object' as that by which it is sustained and which is not at its disposal. At bottom, this is the reason why it can no longer present it as object, because the object is precisely that which is always, in principle, at the disposal of the subject. Among other things, this is what clearly distinguishes Heideggerian *Andenken* from any kind of historicistic coming to awareness.

However, it would be wrong to think, as some interpreters do, that in emphasizing the *Denken/Dank* nexus, Heidegger's desire is to suggest that thinking must find its issue in religion – at least in any conventional sense of the idea. It is not that authentic thought is a thought which thanks; rather, thinking which thinks that which is authentically to be thought is authentic thanks (cf. WT p. 145). That which Dasein most profoundly is and has, and that which is encountered in *Denken/Danken*, is not a gift to be thought of in terms of a being – life, talent, etc. . . – and for which thanks ought to be given. That which Dasein is and has is its ecstatic standing in the disclosedness of Being. The importance of the *Denken/Danken/Gedächtnis* nexus is therefore always to be sought in the fact that thought as memory thinks *Anwesen* as *Anwesenlassen*, as an event of disclosing. What constitutes Dasein – what it is and has – is its relation to disclosure *as an event*.

We can see here a close connection between *Andenken* and the existential analytic of *Being and Time*. To think of disclosing as an event means seeing the open disclosure which constitutes our historical thrownness as precisely a historical disclosure, and not as identical to Being, which is how it is seen by the metaphysics that imposes itself as technology or *Ge-stell* (translatable for that reason as im-position: cf. QT p. 20). Thinking as recollecting in no way means being bound to the past (which is merely another present, one no longer at our disposal): nor does it mean relating in thanks to some presence on which we might depend; rather, it means grasping the disclosure of Being, into which we are thrown, in its eventual nature. Or again, it signifies remembering *Schickung* as *Schic-kung*, as a making present, or facing the totality of the 'founding-founded' of metaphysics deployed in technology as a historical possibility and not as Being itself.

It is no accident that Heidegger introduces *Andenken* in precisely this liberating role towards the end of *Der Satz vom Grund*, when concluding his treatment of the principle of sufficient reason by a reference to the *Ab-grund* and the Heraclitan image of *aiòn* as a divine child playing. Does it look like an arbitrary and illogical game, a sort of coquetry on the part of thinking, to introduce a reference to play at this point? 'So it may seem,' says Heidegger, 'as long as we persist in neglecting to think from the point of view of the *Geschick* of Being, i.e. go on failing to entrust ourselves to the liberating bond that places us in the tradition of thought' (SVG p. 187).

Not only the reference to *Ueberlieferung*, in this case to Heraclitus, allows us to introduce the idea of play; at a deeper level it is the *lösende Bindung* with tradition, to which we entrust ourselves in *Andenken*, that in general allows us to play. This term is highly significant in Heidegger's thought. I do not intend to make a detailed study of the various ways it is understood and developed by him or by thinking that looks to him (Gadamer's for example), but I do want to call attention to two points in particular. First, there is a notion here that is also strongly emphasized by those who interpret Heidegger in relation to Wittgenstein and 'foundationless thinking'. And yet the way the term 'play' is used, in the parts of *Der Satz vom Grund* to which I have referred, gives a very clear idea of the abyssal (*ab-gründlich?*) distance separating Heideggerian play from Wittgenstein's 'game' – defined by the fact that it has rules. In Heidegger, 'play' signifies exactly the opposite of subjection to rules; for him it designates that margin of freedom (cf. the 'play' in a steering-wheel, for example) which does not confirm the rules as much as it suspends them – not in the sense that it invalidates them, but in the sense that it reveals them to be dependent. It reveals them as being *eventual*, as being events, but therefore also possibilities.

Second, this 'image' of the opening of the disclosure of Being, or of the *Uebereignen* in which the *Ereignis* of Being occurs, as play, must not make us forget that there is another important component in the idea of play as Heidegger uses it. It is one which provides a continuity between *Being and Time* and this aspect of the mature Heidegger, and it is in addition the element through which the former thought clarifies the latter. Play is also and above all a *putting into play*. It is risk and uncertainty, but first and foremost it is inseparably bound up with Dasein's being mortal. The play on the basis of which we must think Being as *Ab-grund* is that play 'into which we are brought as mortals, which we are only to the extent that we dwell in proximity to death, which as the utmost possibility of Dasein, makes possible (*vermag*) the highest point of the *Lichtung* of Being and its truth' (SVG pp. 186–7). As also appears in this brief quotation, the guiding thread in the nexus between play and being mortal is not so much the one that relates to the concept of choice and risk, but the one that relates directly to the 'possibilizing' function of death in *Being and Time*. Moreover this function of making possible is a feature of *Andenken* before it is a feature of play. *Andenken* thinks Being *as difference*, i.e. as that which differs/defers in a whole range of senses: first of all in the sense that in the giving it is not given as such, and thus defers as that which flees, that which has been and from which its provenance, in its coming, always also takes its leave; but *Andenken* also always differs as that which is other, that which in its reducibility to open disclosure defers that disclosure insofar as it dis-locates and suspends it (makes it depend, appends it) in its peremptory quality of presence. If we wanted to put all this into the language of *Being and Time*, we could say that *Andenken* is the thought that lets the possible be as possible, stripping it of the mask of necessity imposed on it by metaphysics, the mask which metaphysics forces on it to the highest degree in the final identification of Being with objectness. If *Andenken* can hope to think presence 'properly' as *Anwesenlassen* and difference, that is because it is the thought of Dasein as mortal, of Dasein who 'by anticipation', becomes free *for* [its] own death' (BT p. 308).

To make an explicit connection between *Andenken* and the anticipation of death helps to bring out, both in the notion of *Verstehen* as developed in *Being and Time* and in the idea of recollective thought as elaborated in the later Heidegger, the specific 'ungrounding' quality that distinguishes them. It

125

also throws fresh light on the notion of the hermeneutical circle, so crucial to *Being and Time*. In that work Heidegger's discourse on the hermeneutical circle signifies above all a recognition that every interpretation – and therefore every theoretical or practical thematization of something as something – is always directed in advance by a pre-understanding, which is constitutive of the *Geworfenheit* (thrownness) of Dasein. However, the anticipatory freeing oneself for death is not, in *Being and Time*, explicitly connected to the idea of the hermeneutical circle, except through the discussion of authentic and inauthentic existence. Within certain limits, even this discourse on the hermeneutical circle might still be read in foundational terms: *why* a determinate interpretation and discussion of Being articulated in certain ways was sought in the precomprehension constitutive of the interpreting Dasein's historical thrownness.

When the relation of *Andenken* with being-towards-death is brought out what becomes clarified is also the ungrounding quality of anticipatory resolve with respect to death in *Being and Time*. One consequence is thus also the link between anticipatory resolve and the circularity of the hermeneutical circle. In fact, in *Being and Time* both the anticipation of death and *Andenken* mean that the possibilities of Dasein are suspended in their nature as possibilities. The result of this is on one hand to open the historicity of existence as a hermeneutical *continuum*, allowing Dasein to dis-course from one possibility to another, not being bound definitively to any, but also without making any leaps. Thereby the anticipation of death in some sense also constitutes the concreteness and the texture of subjective life. But on the other hand, the anticipation of death also means that the texture of the historical continuity of existence is suspended in relation to a foundation which is in reality an *Ab-grund* and which is now shown to be totally unfounded. In this sense, the circularity of the hermeneutical circle can become the principle of an 'infinite analysis'. It is precisely this second dimension of the hermeneutical circle and of being-towards-death that emerges with the elaboration of *Andenken*. Here, mortal thinking no longer looks simply like thinking which in leaping forward towards its own death constitutes existence as texture or as continuity of sense, articulated within a totality of instruments. Mortal thinking is thinking which, insofar as it is mortal, responds to the *Zuspruch* of a giving that in the act of giving withdraws, and to which therefore it can relate only through an infinite return. Distinct from memory as a pure faculty of making present, *Andenken* is the thought of infinite return.

This infinite return is *play*, both because it suspends the peremptory seriousness of the texture of existence, moving in a deregulated sphere, and because it puts Dasein into play as mortal. In fact it is as mortal that Dasein accedes to the *Ab-grund* on which any founding-founded contextuality of its history rests. It is being-towards-death that unmasks the historical *continuum* as ultimately marked by discontinuity, that of the *Ab-grund*. A rigorous reading should be given in these terms to expressions like 'death is the shrine of nothing' (PLT p. 178). Dasein thinks Being as difference solely to the extent that it is projected towards its own death.

But the fact that the relation to the *Ab-grund* is linked to being-mortal means something else as well, namely, that such a relation to the *Ab-grund* is always also articulated as a relation to the past, from which Dasein as mortal actually emerges. *Andenken* is also therefore memory in the literal sense, the sense of a historiographical going back over the *Ueberlieferung*. Recollective thought is hermeneutical thought, and to think Being as *Anwesenlassen* means to recall its nature as event by retracing it in the 'concatenation of events'. This Heidegger does when he retraces the history of metaphysics, the history of key words like *a-létheia*, *Grund*, *logos* and suchlike. But this retracing has objectives that are diametrically opposed to those of *Historie* as a positioning or founding of actual historical circumstances through the elucidation of their conditions in the past. What *Andenken* does as hermeneutical thought is in fact constantly to unground the historical contexts to which it applies itself, subjecting the 'words' that constitute these to infinite analysis. It is to this ungrounding characteristic of the Heideggerian hermeneutic that we can quite fairly relate that contemporary hermeneutical ontology which considers 'inexhaustibility' to be a feature of Being and truth, and founds an ever-open infinity of interpretation upon it.[5]

This hermeneutical return *in infinitum* overturns the prescriptions of logic, and never has any 'constructive' ends, at least in the usual sense of the term. But ungrounding claims a radical constructivity to the extent that, by suspending the peremptoriness and cogency of each of the different contexts into which historical existence is thrown, it liberates Dasein for other contexts. The riskiness that belongs to the game can be seen in the fact that liberation from the exclusive bond to its historical context puts Dasein itself in a state of suspension; a suspension which touches him in his deepest constitution as subject (and it is in this sense that I believe Heidegger's antisubjectivism is to be read).

What then can be said for the continuity that constitutes subjective life (even on a psychological level), when the latter turns out to be marked in its very structure by the discontinuity of the *Ab-grund*? Are we not in the very same situation described by Nietzsche in *The Gay Science*, when he speaks in aphorism 54 about 'the consciousness that I am dreaming and that I must go on dreaming'? Nietzsche's work clearly shows that all this has vast implications for the mode of thinking the I as individuality/identity.

In the light of this analysis of *Andenken*, the thinking that thinks Being 'properly' comes to mean a thinking that plays leaping towards the *Ab-grund*, that stakes or brings into play[6] both itself and all the contexts of its historical existence in an infinite analysis. This analysis is extremely hard for logic to digest, but equally it is an analysis that is disappointing, embarrassing and worrying for anyone who expects from Heidegger a theory of disalienation. Kostas Axelos, for instance, writes: 'Heidegger has a theory of human alienation, but not of disalienation.'[7] If what I have said so far is valid, then the truth is that in Heidegger alienation, if it really merits that name, has no need of being suppressed or overcome. The *Schicken* of Being is such that, in its giving, it withholds and withdraws as giving. No thinking relation with Being thus understood as difference is possible other than one of recollection and in some sense of 'leave-taking' and this means – if the term is appropriate – an alienated relation. (Alienation is also what is seen in the *Denken/Dank* nexus, which implies a dispossession of man, just as *Ereignis* as *Uebereignen* is dispossessing.) Disalienation might mean a situation in which Being as such is finally given in presence. That this in fact must be so seems clear to me in the light of the Classicist origins of alienation/disalienation discourse. This discourse always operates within the horizon traced out by the Winckelmannian/Schillerian model of ideal humanity as harmonized totality. The disalienated man is the man who becomes most like a Greek statue, in which is actualized the perfect coincidence of internal and external, as Hegel puts it so definitively in his *Aesthetics*, and in which there thus remains nothing unsaid (even though the Greek statue does not speak; but it does not need to talk any more, and *Sprache* moreover has a privileged connection in Heidegger with being-mortal). This horizon of disalienation as the idealization of presence unfolded in a harmonized totality, something that is typical of virtually all of contemporary Marxist thought, is also the locus for the recuperation of Heidegger in terms of 'foundationless thinking'. For such thinking, 'abandoning Being as foundation' does not signify making oneself ready for the leap towards the *Ab-grund*; it means corresponding to the call of the principle of reason without reserve and without any residuum (without anything being left unsaid).

Over against the ideal of disalienation, Heidegger sets an (implicit) ideal of 'authentic' humanity which refers to terms such as being-toward-death or to the *Geviert*, the framework for the unfolding of the relations between earth and heaven, men and gods.[8] The way to pick out these elements of the Heideggerian 'image of man' is perhaps to make a close study of Heidegger's readings of poets, paying special attention to their particular 'contents'. Possibly because of his disdain for 'popular' existentialism, Heidegger always discouraged 'existential' readings of his work. As a result, to my knowledge, no research on such lines has ever been undertaken on any really significant level. But an inquiry of this kind ought to demonstrate how mistaken is the (rarely confessed) stereotype of a Heidegger obsessed with an ideal of Black Forest agricultural/pastoral humanity, living according to the natural rhythms of day and night, birth and death. The investigation I have in mind would show instead that what dominates Heidegger's thinking is the effort to formulate an understanding of human existence on a model entirely distinct from the Classicist one predominant since the Renaissance (on the level of artistic, philosophical and political expression at least). *En passant*, it is worth noting the Classicist features in totalitarian ideologies.

In this sense it would be only slightly provocative to suggest a contrast between Heidegger and Schiller, with Heidegger at least at this point carrying on the revolution against Classicism initiated by Nietzsche in *The Birth of Tragedy*. We would need to examine how far the Nietzschean Dionysiac theme may also be found in Heidegger in two of its senses at least: the inclusion of the capacity for suffering in the ideal of an 'authentic' existence (in Heidegger the man of 'the desert that grows' has lost even the capacity to suffer); and the ungrounding of the *principium individuationis*, taken equally to mean the ungrounding of the subject. In the light of all this we ought also to reopen discussion of Heidegger's own view of Nietzsche and recognize the affinity between them. 'Heidegger contra Schiller' as an interpretative key makes all the more sense if other similarly remarkable contrasting pairings important for twentieth-century culture are borne in mind. I am thinking of those that offer, over against the Classicist ideal of disalienation, a conception of the negative according to which the negative cannot be included and liquidated in the perspective of a possible final 'redemption'. Examples would include the alternatives that could be recognized between Bataille and Breton (see Perniola's book on Bataille),[9] Adorno and Marcuse, and maybe Benjamin and Bloch. In all these alternatives, in which negative thought, to quote Bataille, remains an 'old mole' (the mole of Marx's revolution) and never becomes a 'supereagle',[10] may lie a hint for research along the lines suggessted by Heidegger's notion of *Andenken*.

All the themes I have discussed, and especially these last ones, necessarily require further development, so that any conclusions must be very provisional at this stage: but tentatively perhaps I might at least put forward two propositions:

1   Although my stress on the theme of thinking as *Andenken* cannot of course serve to project or achieve anything like a global transformation of 'culture', it is still not without implications and effects on that level. For its tendency is to conceive the human sciences in a manner that is not subject to the model of the natural sciences or to the ends of unconditional technological domination of the world. It assumes that the production of meanings follows an autonomous logic, not reducible to the logic of the production of the instruments of existence, even though it is not necessarily in conflict with it, and even if it rejects any kind of hegemonic claim like the one that dominated the ideal of philosophy proper to metaphysics, a hegemony that, in the epoch of accomplished metaphysics, has caused subjugation

to another hegemony, that of technological reason, still conceived as a sovereign reason and the locus of meaning. The perspective I am proposing focuses on hermeneutics, which does not necessarily mean a sovereignty of historiography or philology. Such a sovereignty represents yet another misunderstanding of the meaning of *Andenken*, whereby it is identified purely and simply with historical memory and ultimately with *Historie*. Hermeneutical thinking by contrast is, in another and perhaps more legitimate sense, that knowledge that is unfolding today in the critique of ideology[11] and in psychoanalysis, which, however, must be engaged in explicitly from the hermeneutical viewpoint as a methodological model of 'infinite analysis', free from any tendency to be equated with a mere instrument of an 'awareness' that is still subjectivistic and metaphysical. In a perspective of hermeneutical thinking as an infinite analysis of the backgrounds conditioning every context of meaning, there fall away even the rigid distinctions between thinking as 'reflection' and thinking as exercised in the production of art. Especially in the form it has assumed since the modern avant-garde, art is an eminent mode of infinite analysis. And perhaps this is where we should seek one of the meanings of the dialogue proposed by Heidegger between thinking and poeticizing.

2   The centrality of technology in Heidegger's mature thought should not be read as a call to respond unreservedly to the technical provocation; perhaps (on the basis of a rather ingenuous dialectic) in the hope that if technology is pushed to its most extreme point on the level of the conditions of production and the resulting forms of social organization, this will at the same time necessarily lead to an overcoming of the 'desert' that technology brings with it. A *Zuspruch* – an appeal that is at the same time an encouragement – resounds in technology, as in the principle of sufficient reason; it resounds alongside the call of that principle to which calculative

reason responds by subjecting itself to it. Reflective thought must respond to this *Zuspruch* by risking a leap into the *Abgrund*. But in respect of this leap, what 'positive' meaning can be attributed to the fact that today metaphysics has in fact reached its end in the total technological organization of the world? In what sense is it true that 'where danger is grows the saving power also'?[12] The way 'foundationless thinking' responds to this fact is not convincing, nor is the ingenuously dialectical response which expects the overcoming of technical thought to follow directly from its own extremity. Equally, I see nothing different in general terms about the recent suggestion[13] that technology, by deploying representational thought in its pure representationality and making it a mere 'double' of the existent, would definitively unmask its ideological character and thus free thinking to adopt another position in regard to Being. Can we really imagine that the culmination of metaphysics in technology is preparing the way for another epoch of Being? Can thinking as *Andenken* actually mark an epoch in the way that metaphysical thinking has managed to do? Surely it is a constitutive feature of *Andenken* that it *cannot become* the principle of a total organization of beings, and thus must inevitably always be restricted in this sense too to playing the part of an 'old mole'?

The relation between deployed technology and the possibility that thinking may be able to put itself into a position of *Andenken* cannot be direct: *andenkend* thinking is not to be identified with technological thinking, nor is it prepared for by technological thinking, in the sense of being the dialectical outcome of technological thinking. The relation between *Andenken* and technology can only be oblique. This means that, like Bataille's 'old mole', *andenkend* thought rests within calculative thinking, itself hearing the call of the principle of sufficient reason, but deliberately misunderstanding it, that is, understanding it – as Heidegger shows in the lectures on *Der Satz vom Grund* – by stressing in another way that which this reason leaves unsaid. Not '*Nothing* is *without* foundation', but 'Nothing *is* without *foundation*' (SVG p. 204). If we lay the stress here, it opens the way to hearing in a *seinsgeschicklich* manner the coincidence of Being and *Grund*, and it therefore prepares for the leap towards the *Ab-Grund*. The whole way in which *andenkend* thinking hears the metaphysical tradition has this mark of obliqueness, which in the Heideggerian texts chiefly takes the form of hermeneutical dis-location, as lost-ness, *Unheimlichkeit* or disorientation, which might equally be thought of in Klossowskian terms as parody.

On the historical level this may mean that *andenkend* thinking, rejecting the call to the attribution of sufficient reason, rejecting the call to submit to the dominion of technical thought, manages to make a niche for itself in the interstices of this dominion, like the underclass which, living on social security in Western cities, is a necessary by-product of those cities. In this way *andenkend* thinking may paradox-ically establish a 'positive' relation towards the technical. But is there really such a clear distinction between a strong technological society and a society of its by-products? Does it not imply, sociologically, a doubtful mythology, namely, a humanity entirely devoted to the technical domination of the world, living the technological imperatives to the full, like those Russian Stakhanovites who lived to the utmost the imperatives of 'revolutionary' productivity? Over against this mythical figure of the technical man, the pure 'worker' (who is not necessarily 'exploited' but who is certainly more or less an automaton), is set another, no less mythical figure, that of the man of the underclass as the ultimate refined *flâneur*, who, precisely because he assumes an active relation with the technical world, will probably not even have the ability to nestle in the interstices of technology, in the holes of the rational net. Might there not be a more complex relationship, given that the *Zuspruch* of Being is grasped only when we are also able to hear (though not exclusively) the *Anspruch* of the principle of sufficient reason? Furthermore, insofar as *andenkend* thinking seems unable to give rise to an epoch of Being or a global organization of beings, it is also probably unable itself to inform a class or a social group of which it might be the patrimony and the principle of legitimation, not even when the social group in question is defined purely negatively, like the underclass (although in Marx the proletariat is defined negatively too). If that is so, then maybe the 'old mole' of *Andenken* can also and perhaps especially make its niche in the technical class itself, as the permanent instance of the ungrounding of its own existence. (As Nietzsche put it, 'What do I matter?' is written on the door of the future thinker'.[14]) But whether *Andenken* has its historical home in the centre of cities or on their outskirts, is a question that cannot be decided theoretically, and it may not even be important theoretically. What theory can be sure of is that the relation between *Andenken* and technology can only be an oblique one. How this obliqueness might be further but not exclusively articulated on a historical level must remain an open question. And perhaps precisely for that reason the question of technology needs to be raised repeatedly by *andenkend* thinking.

Notes

1   Cf. esp. the writings of Massimo Cacciari, beginning with *Krisis*, Milan, 1976, and *Pensiero negativo e razionalizzazione*, Venice, 1977.

2   Analogies with the kind of approach adopted by Cacciari may be found in studies on Heidegger like those of K. Axelos; see his *Marx e Heidegger*, trans. and ed. E. Mazzarella, Naples, 1978; *Einführung in ein künftiges Denken*, Tübingen, 1966, *Arguments d'une recherche*, Paris, 1969.

3   Vattimo is here playing on two meanings of the Italian word *differire* (to defer/differ) and following Derrida's own practice with the similar French word *différer*. (Translator's note.)

4   Vattimo is here quoting from a sentence in the German text

of *Was heisst Denken?* that is omitted from the English translation: 'Andenken ist anderes als die fluchtige Vergegenwartigung von Vergangenen' (Tübingen, 1954, p. 159).

5 In this connection, see L. Pareyson, *Verità e Interpretazione*, Milan, 1971.

6 'Mette in gioco': this also means 'stakes' or 'sets at risk'. (Translator's note.)

7 K. Axelos, *Arguments d'une recherche*, p. 101.

8 On the *Geviert*, see esp. the lecture on 'The Thing' in Heidegger's *Poetry, Language, Thought*, trans. A. Hofstadter, New York, 1971, pp. 163ff.

9 M. Perniola, *G. Bataille e il negativo*, Milan, 1977.

10 See G. Bataille, 'La *vieille taupe* et le préfixe *sur* dans les mots *surhomme* et *surrealisme*', in *Oeuvres complètes*, vol. II, Paris, 1970, pp. 93–109.

11 I use the term in the sense that it is used not only by Habermas but also by K. O. Apel, *Towards a transformation of Philosophy*, trans. G. Adey and D. Frisby, London, 1980; although in my view Apel's thought needs to be radicalized in the direction I have suggested in my introduction to the Italian translation of his book: K. O. Apel, *Comunità e comunicazione*, trans. G. Carchio, Turin, 1977.

12 These are two lines from Hölderlin that Heidegger often dwells on, for example, in QT p. 28.

13 By Eugenio Mazzarella in the introduction to K. Axelos, *Marx e Heidegger*; this piece is a penetrating essay in Heideggerian interpretation.

14 *Daybreak*, p. 547.

6

The Adventure of Difference

IN exploring the history of philosophy, Heidegger showed that the inheritance we receive from a given thinker is the nucleus he leaves us of what is still to be thought, not acquired results but ways thinking feels called on to follow again and again. Is ontological difference, which Heidegger undoubtedly held to be quite central to his own thought, a nucleus of this kind? Ontological difference seems of late to have been following a downward curve, especially in relation to what has been called the philosophy of difference, a particular feature of French philosophical culture since Derrida. It is not simply that in recent times the subject of difference as discussed by authors like Derrida, Deleuze and Foucault has undergone, on the level of a chronology or sociology of culture, something of an eclipse in its popularity (probably connected with the decline in fashion of structuralism, with which it does have certain limited affinities). Even on the level of theoretical development there seem to be various signs that the idea of difference, having run round the whole curve of its possibilities, is declining and fading away into other philosophical standpoints. Jacques Derrida's 1968 Paris lecture on *différance*[1] may at the time have looked like a straight manifesto of the philosophy of difference, but today it looks more like a kind of epitaph or memorial for it.

Even at the time of its delivery this discourse was sympto-
matic and indicative of the decline of difference. (Is this too
perhaps a peculiar destiny of difference, an 'effect of difference'?) If we retrace the theoretical path followed by thinkers
like Derrida and Deleuze, this decline looks inevitable. But
my point is that this phenomenon is very far from signifying
any decline in or exhaustion of the idea of ontological
difference put forward by Heidegger; it is precisely in such
adventures and in such a dissolution of 'the philosophy of
difference' that ontological difference taps into its still-
productive core, a core that constitutes an authentic future
for thinking.

At the end of his 1968 lecture Derrida distanced himself
from Heidegger; if we analyse closely how he did this, we
can observe at one and the same time the reasons for both the
decline of difference (and Derridean *différance*) and the 'persistence' of Heideggerian ontological difference. First of all,
Derrida exhibited the play of two meanings of the term
difference, which he spelt *différance*, wishing thereby to show
how the differential element that constitutes the sign is not at
the same time something that can be grasped as 'different'.
(Of course it needs to be borne in mind that in French the
sound of the word remains the same whether it is written
with an *e* or an *a*.) Derrida then went on to show how the
two meanings that the word *différer* has in French – 'being
distinct or divergent' and 'deferring' in time – play a crucial
role for some great thinkers of difference, such as Nietzsche,
Freud, Levinas and above all Heidegger. Finally, Derrida
asked whether his idea of difference could in some way be
related to what Heidegger calls ontological difference, the
difference between Being and beings. Although Derrida is
aware of deep connections between his notion and Heidegger's ontological difference conceived as the difference between Being and beings, the latter seems to Derrida to
remain imprisoned within the horizon of metaphysics, or at
least within a metaphysical nostalgia. He thinks some confir-

mation of this nostalgia may be found, for example, in the part of Heidegger's *Holzwege* that deals with Anaximander. Derrida comments on a few sentences in this which assign to thinking the clearly impossible task of 'finding a single word, the single word . . . to name the essence of Being', and therefore the relation of presence to a present being.[2] But to think of the possibility of finding the single word to name the essence of Being is still to be thinking in terms of full presence. For Derrida, however, the philosophy of difference signifies above all a recognition 'that there has never been and never will be a single word, a *master-name*',[3] for difference is prior to everything. 'In the beginning was the trace' we might say, to sum up Derrida's position in a sentence. A trace, then, and never a presence to which the trace can be related; for the differences that structure the field of human experience originate from the start in a difference, a difference that is at the same time divergence and indefinite deferment, and in which what is there beforehand is always a trace and never an original. But it is such an original that ought to be named by the single word, by the supreme proper and non-metaphorical term. The scope of Derrida's development of this declension of the concept of difference is well-known, especially his polemic against phenomenology as thinking that privileges presence, the giving of essences in flesh and blood, the preference for *phoné* over *grammé*. It is as though presence summed up in itself all the 'authoritarian' features of metaphysics as (alleged) knowledge of first principles. In setting difference against presence, Derrida wants therefore to destroy the authoritarianism of the *archai*. This is exactly why difference cannot presume to be another name to indicate origin; nor can talk of differences which assumes them to be the centre of a constellation of other ideas be legitimized by reference to such an origin, in the way that metaphysical discourse draws its validity from the fact of being able to state principles. Talk of difference can in fact be only a totally arbitrary decision, a 'gamble' that for

Derrida responds to 'a strategy without objectives' or 'blind tactics' that relate only to play.

And yet there is a contrast between the emphasis placed on the choice of difference as pure play and the affirmation to be found on the same pages that there is a 'correspondence' between difference and the present situation of thinking. The idea of defference looks like 'the most proper one to think, if not to master . . . what is most irreducible about our "era" '.[4] This is a 'small contradiction', one might call it a 'wrinkle' or a margin in the Derridean text, and yet underneath it a far from marginal question is being smuggled away. The question is: 'who and what makes such a difference?' All Heidegger's thinking on difference, for example, may be read as the development of a problem Derrida never stops for a second to consider – the problem of how difference can seem to be the most appropriate term for conceiving our epoch. The fact is determined by reference to the metaphysical oblivion of Being, and so by reference to the distance of thought from that *Frühe* in which this oblivion has not as yet been rigidified in the forms of accomplished metaphysics; and by reference to the possibility that another epoch might follow that of metaphysics thus defined, another kind of connection between man and the relations between presence and being-that-is-present. These are the various features of what Heidegger calls the *eventual* nature of Being, which vanish completely in the Derridean interpretation of the idea of difference.

According to Derrida, all the differences internal to the differential relation between Being and beings, and in the first place this difference itself, ontological difference, name something that cannot have a name. ' "Older" than Being itself, such a *différance* has no name in our language.' We are not talking here about a lack or a defect in language; in reality, 'there is no *name* for it at all, not even the name of essence or of Being, not even that of *différance*, which is not a name, which is not a pure nominal unity, and unceasingly dislocates itself in a chain of differing and deferring substitutions.'[5] The moment difference is enunciated it disappears, it declines, becoming identified with the differences that effectively constitute the concatenation of the signifier. To name difference is merely to open up the system of differences that constitutes the symbolic in its effective differential structure; it discloses differences as *différance*, that is, as *simulacra*.

The difference produced by the gamble that chooses to say *différance* is both important and insignificant at the same time: it shows differences in their purely differential character, i.e. as *traces* for which there has never been a corresponding presence, and therefore precisely as simulacra. But to say *différance* in this way makes no difference, inasmuch as the differential structure that characterizes the symbolic is left to be what it has always been, and yet, in its totality the symbolic has also been revealed as a pure system of simulacra, traces without originals, and is thus subjected to a kind of *epoché* or suspension of that metaphysical assent that the *archai* have always claimed in the sphere of the representative mentality.

If difference does not have a name, it none the less seems both in Derrida's theoretical statements and even more so in his actual practice of thinking, that there are certain ways it is given, certain dislocations, that are not strictly equivalent to each other:

> Always differing and deferring, the trace is never as it is in the presentation of itself. It erases itself in presenting itself, muffles itself in resonating. The annunciatory and reserved trace of this movement can always be disclosed in metaphysical discourse, and especially in the contemporary discourse which states, through the attempts to which we just referred (Nietzsche, Freud, Lévinas), the closure of ontology, and especially through the Heideggerian text.[6]

In the text of metaphysics, and that means in every text characterized by the trace and by the disappearance of the trace, there are wrinkles, margins, zones in which the trace of this movement of disappearance is easier to pick up. As a retracing thought (picking up traces, but also reducing everything to a trace) the philosophy of difference works on texts by searching in them for what Derrida elsewhere calls *undecidables*: terms, ideas, simulacrum concepts such as, for instance, *pharmakon*, supplement, hymen, mark/margin and, of course, *différance* itself. Terms like these make the difference without in their turn being differentiable, decidable and distinguishable from others. Working on undecidables, as Derrida does, means deconstructing the text of metaphysics by showing that the oppositions in terms of which it is articulated are only differences. They are at once less and more than oppositions: less, inasmuch as the opposed terms are given *not* in relation to a fractured primordial structure, but only by virtue of a de-cision, a gamble, which constitutes them as oppositions without foundation; but this de-cision is not the place for a possible reconciliation, for it is a non-place, in its turn a pure trace of an original that is not given and cannot be given, and in this sense the undecidable reveals that the opposition is more than opposition, since it shows it to be insuperable. Duality irreducible to unity is thus infected with a delirium that multiplies it in a process without end. In spite of this delirium, however, undecidables remain a kind of privileged place in which the movement of difference as *différance* can be rehearsed.

Such are the two characteristic features of the Derridean philosophy of difference: first, *différance* is unnamable as such; it shows itself only in the moment when it declines into the infinitely open chain of differences, the simulacra that constitute the history of Western culture and of every culture, insofar as we can no longer talk of an epoch of metaphysics or of particular moments within it once the Heideggerian articulations of the history of Being have been abandoned. Second, even if only in a very limited sense, it is possible to 'speak' *différance* by working on undecidables; it is what 'makes the difference' and distinguishes Derridean writing from that of the metaphysical texts it aims to deconstruct. But precisely as a function of the first of these points, it is possible to speak difference only by remaining within metaphysics in such a way as to erode its margins, or rather, to rewrite the text of metaphysics *parodistically*. The philosophy of difference has an eminently contemplative character; in fact it unfolds as a pure parodistic reduplication of metaphysics precisely insofar, as a matter of principle, as it cannot fail to share the status of simulacrum that is character-istic of every metaphysical text, and indeed definitively of texts in general. The distinguishing mark of deconstructive thought is merely a different attitude in the exercise of the play of simulacra, or, in other words, a different position of consciousness, the production of simulacra or metaphors that are aware of being such.

All this can be seen expounded and perhaps oversimplified in those of Derrida's disciples who have devoted themselves to the interpretation of the works of Nietzsche,[7] in their eyes the initiator of this practice of parodistically rewriting the metaphysical text. Parody is the only way of 'making the difference' in a situation in which all differentiation is always only the process of duplicating the trace, that is a situation in which the absolutization of difference has taken away all possibility of differentiation. But parody is defined solely in terms of a position of consciousness and this is a classic element in the arsenal of metaphysics and of presential thinking. This return of consciousness corresponds merely to the 'return' of another classic element in the thought of presence, the idea of structure. Speaking of the Nietzschean figures of Apollo and Dionysus in his 1963 essay 'Force and Signification', Derrida writes that the divergence between Apollo and Dionysus, or rather the internal difference that works Dionysus himself as a divergence between *élan* and structure, 'is not *in* history. It too, in an unexpected sense, is

143

an original structure.'[8] Both Derrida's predilection for structural linguistics, so explicit in his essay on *La différance*, and for Lacanian psychoanalysis, take him further in the direction of a metaphysical rigidification of the idea of difference. Even if only in a somewhat unusual sense, *différance* is in every respect an archstructure, diametrically opposed to Heideggerian ontological difference as an aspect of the eventuality and therefore also of the historicity of Being. *Différance* as archstructure is not in history, it never comes to pass, but then again constitutes a return to the most classic qualification of metaphysical Being, eternity. (Whether this be an eternity of the trace, an eternity that is not homogeneous, or an eternity marked by an irremediable absence, it does not offer an alternative to metaphysics.)

Thus in Derrida *différance* seems to dissolve through its own absolutization, which tends to confer on it again the very features of metaphysical Being. Gilles Deleuze, on the other hand, starting from the same premises as Derrida, moves towards the eradication of any possibility of an equivocal return to structures and metaphysics.

Of the two poles between which Derridean difference moves – archstructure and simulacrum – Deleuze isolates the second. For him, repetition is not repetition of a primordial difference or first trace, but gives rise itself to the only difference, that is, to the ever diverse differences of simulacra. From the start, Deleuze attributes to difference the same meaning as Derrida: it means that every alleged immediacy is always already a duplication, the duplication of an original that is not there. 'To overturn Platonism,' he writes, means 'to deny the primacy of an original over its copy, or of a model over its picture. It means to glorify the reign of simulacra and reflections.'[9] This is also the meaning that Derrida attributes to his own idea of an archtrace. However, for him the idea does not have only this meaning. Derrida's stress on undecidables, on those zones in the text of metaphysics where difference's movement from appearance to disappearance is most readily discernible, signifies that this thought has a further sense beyond that of a bare negation of any form of presence of the origin. To be distinguished from metaphysical thinking pure and simple, and therefore also from the thought of presence, deconstructive thinking must necessarily refer to an archstructure; even when such a reference can be made only as a parodistic rewriting of the metaphysical text, the position of the consciousness constituting the parody exists only insofar as it opposes to unconscious differences a sort of primal *différance*. But if on the other hand difference is affirmed as the universality of the simulacrum or of a duplication that has no model, every distinction between simulacra, every hierarchy among traces is arbitrary, and if not explicitly acknowledged as such, only reproduces metaphysical mythologies. On this basis, in the work he wrote in collaboration with Guattari, *Anti-Oedipus*,[10] Deleuze undertakes a radical critique of Marx and Freud; for although they lay the foundations for the unmasking of the real as simulacrum (ideology or sublimation), at the same time they 'recodify' privileged sites of its constitution: the economy of the relations of production, the economy of familial relations. Even Lacan, who according to Deleuze made a crucial move in liberating Freudian recodification from its mythical tinsel (Oedipus), in separating the function of the Father from the real father and the Phallus from the penis, still clings to a rigid structure of symbolic functions.[11] Thus Deleuze's polemic against psychoanalysis and Marxism is again a variation of the interpretation of difference as a purification of the simulacrum from all structural reference.

What has happened to difference here? Is there any sense in which we can still apply the phrase 'philosophy of difference' to a philosophy of the simulacrum that glorifies the duplication operated by a libido with no canalization or code on a 'body without organs'? Perhaps so, but only on condition that difference becomes a question of pure energy, assimilable to that inequality of forces which creates the possibility of fluxes, the exchange processes of life. This is in fact the outcome of Deleuze's thought, and it is strongly suggestive of a return to Bergsonian vitalism, a constant source of inspiration for his work. As long as difference is reduced to nothing more than an indication of the inequalities that make possible the movements of life, there is no real discussion of the other difference, the difference between the institution and the de-stitution of codes. Vitalism is at work here, in the sense that the alternation of codification and de-territorialization, of canalizing rigidification and the liberation of fluxes, is simply referred back to life and its rhythms, without a real discussion of the problem.

The dissolution of difference both in Derrida and Deleuze refers legitimately to key aspects in the Nietzschean philosophy of eternal recurrence. Difference as archstructure of an infinite process of repetition is eternal recurrence understood as a law of Being, as fate, as a negation of Judaeo-Christian, linear historicity in favour of a Greek type of circularity. Difference as a glorification of the simulacrum is rather the dance and the laugh of Zarathustra, recurrence as the innocence of becoming, the Will to Power.[12]

However, these two aspects of eternal recurrence are ones that Zarathustra brands as features of a partial and superficial interpretation of the idea. When his animals put forward the idea of recurrence in the form of the eternally recurring dance of all things, his response is: 'O you buffoons and barrel-organs—. . . you – have already made a hurdy-gurdy song of it' (pp. 234–5). What the animals have transformed into a ditty is the suffering that Zarathustra had to endure in biting the head off the snake that crawled into his mouth.[13] This is the same snake that appears in 'the vision and the riddle' in this third part of *Zarathustra*; here too the shepherd into whose mouth the snake has crawled has to free himself by biting off its head. This bite is the moment of the institution of eternal recurrence; and it is this that is repressed and disappears in the interpretation of eternal recurrence put forward by the philosophy of difference. This bite, and Nietzsche's probable intention in using such an image, certainly cannot be identified with a pure and simple parodistic rewriting of metaphysics, definitively canonizing the archstructure of difference by making it the object of a Spinozistic consciousness. Nor can it be identified with the glorification of the simulacrum, in which even the final differentiating element of Derridean *différance*, the distinguishing of an archstructure, is suppressed in favour of the mere practice of difference as indefinite repetition.

By contrast, it seems to me that if we leave aside all psychological or voluntaristic connotations, the de-cisive meaning of the Nietzschean parable is not repressed in the Heideggerian conception of ontological difference, and I believe this is what makes the difference between Heidegger and the philosophy of difference (or of the dissolution of difference). The crucial distinction is precisely the one mentioned by Derrida in the conclusion of his lecture on *La différance* referred to above. In his effort to think ontological difference, Heidegger is inspired by nostalgia for a relation with Being distinct from the forgetting that is characteristic of metaphysical thought. This is not, of course, the nostalgia for a self-offering of Being in the dimension of presence. The essence of the Being that ought to be named by the word, as discussed in the essay on Anaximander, is a *Wesen* that is always already the *Ereignis* of the establishment of a relation of difference between Being and beings. Naming difference, or as Heidegger puts it elsewhere, 'thinking difference *as* difference' (ID p. 47) does not mean becoming aware of a structure in repeating it. The worry that to name difference by calling it ontological difference already amounts to a relapse into the horizon of metaphysics leads to the evacuation of all content from difference and effectively to its losing all distinction. If the difference in question is not one between Being and beings we are faced with a mere affirmation, and a metaphysical one at that, of the non-homogeneity of that which metaphysics calls real, one or Being. This non-homogeneity is – or is differentiated, is given, unfolds – since the beginning and for ever. All that can change is the attitude of consciousness towards it; rather than accepting Being as homogeneous, the point is to deconstruct it. But deconstruction is not part of difference, for difference as archstructure is always deployed and available; deconstruction is concerned rather with the speculative and representative relation that metaphysics has always established between Being and thought. In Heidegger's eyes, however, the fact that difference is ontological, that it concerns Being in its relation with beings, means rather that this relation, and therefore Being itself, encloses even and above all the mode in which Dasein relates to difference. Difference is the history of Being, it is eventuality: as such it involves man, and concerns him in *Brauch*, in that 'maintenance' by which Heidegger translates Anaximander's *chreon*.

What can it mean – for man and his history, and for the history of Being as the event of Being (and not as the repetition of an immutable archstructure) – to think difference as difference? The word Heidegger uses most consistently to describe this type of thinking is *An-denken*. The chief meaning of *An-denken* is remembrance, memory, recollection. *An-denken* is the thinking that, in recalling difference, recalls Being. This is not, however, a recollection that makes present something which was but is no longer present, it is not an 'ephemeral presencing of the past'. We cannot recall Being in the sense of making present once more, since it has never been present; recalling it has more to do with taking one's leave of it (*verabschieden*) (WT p. 146). Up to this point it looks as if the philosophy of difference as a philosophy of the trace remains faithful to the Heideggerian reading. But what interests Heidegger in the idea of *An-denken* is certainly not merely the affirmation of a primordial absence that constitutes Being by de-stituting it. If we look at what prompted Heidegger in *Being and Time* to initiate the thinking about difference that he was to develop substantially in later years, we can see that his concern (as Gadamer points out in *Truth and Method*)[14] is to locate the Husserlian problematic of constitution in a domain which overcomes transcendentalism definitively. What is given in presence to a knowing subject is given to him within a horizon that is not the horizon of the transcendental I, it is a historically constituted horizon, thrown and finite. The place where Heidegger becomes aware for the first time of ontological difference is the non-coincidence between the horizon of presence and Being as present being; this non-coincidence is at the basis of the relation Heidegger marks out between Being and time. It is something that comes out clearly in his subsequent writings when he talks about the need to conceive *Anwesen* as *An-wesen-lassen* (cf. TB p. 5). It is not so much that by reducing Being to beings, metaphysical thought forgets difference as a structure of absence that is both constitutive and de-stitutive of all presence. Rather, it forgets the making-present that governs and makes possible every determinate presence. From this point of view, ontological difference coincides with Dasein's finitude and historical thrownness. The importance already attributed to hermeneutics in *Being and Time*, and then increasingly in subsequent works, gives a clear enough indication of the direction taken by Heidegger in his efforts to find a thinking that would recollect Being and difference. If Being is given and occurs as the institution of historical horizons within which Dasein encounters beings, and if it is in this way deployed as temporality, then to think Being by recollecting it means above all to relocate that which is present within those horizons that governs it in its being-present. This collocation (*Er-örterung*) is the recollective thought which can be substituted for metaphysics and its claim that it defines all the structures of Being once and for all. Hermeneutical *Er-örterung* is thinking that cor-responds to Being as *event*.

But what is the purpose of *Andenken*? Why should we think *An-wesen* as *An-wesen-lassen* rather than reducing presence to being-that-is-present? In *Being and Time* Heidegger is still deeply moved by the effort to grasp the *ursprünglich* in every phenomenon, and this 'primordiality' is given only when we grasp the totality of the phenomenon in question (which is how, for instance, the discussion of being-unto-death is introduced). The search for the totality of the structures of the phenomenon, and above all those of Dasein, has however a double significance, illustrated by two of the meanings of the term 'drift' – 'meaning' and 'direction'.[15] Striving to grasp the drift of each phenomenon, and in particular the drift of Being as the horizon within which the constitutive structures of beings are given, and hence as the totality of what is available to knowledge, Heidegger discovers the drift of Being to be the *direction* in which Dasein is drawn away from any centre, in a dispossession he sees Being as a drift in which Dasein moves without being able to find a fixed point. The primary meaning of the search for the drift of Being is evident in the stress in *Being and Time* on ideas like those of authenticity and decision: the point is to grasp the prevailing horizon so as not to be 'placed' within it passively any longer, and above all so as to avoid being staked by the uncritical assumptions of the anonymous 'they'. As a first approximation, then, we may say that recollecting the difference between Being and beings means appropriating the horizon within which we are thrown. Although we never grasp it completely, of course, the research of primordial structures, totality, decision and authenticity in *Being and Time* shows that this is broadly the direction in which Heidegger is moving.

From this point of view it is understandable that the outcome of thinking about ontological difference should be hermeneutical thought, understood as the effort to constitute the drift of that which is present on the basis of its connections with past and future. But that which allows Dasein to be constituted as a totality, both as a continuity of individual existence and as a continuity of this with other existences, is its constitutive capacity for dying. The ownmost possibility of Dasein – that of the disappearance of all other possibilities – also constitutes the various possibilities that are given on this side of that one in their very nature as possibilities, conferring on existence the capacity for passing from one to the other in a *discursus* that makes it possible as unitary texture. The possibilities that are presented to Dasein in the *continuum* of individual existence are always in their turn linked to what is commonly called history (they are, for example, conditions, professions, works, languages, together with their specific contexts, developments and destinies) and this is always by virtue of the historicity of Dasein opened by its own being-towards-death.

The hermeneutics that interprets all these components of facticity is very far from that deconstruction of the metaphysical text to which the philosophy of difference devotes itself, repetitively retracing the basic structure of absence. Nor is this hermeneutic to be identified with the delirious production of more and more new simulacra, without any rootedness or 'responsibility'. In the Heideggerian hermeneutic, the bond with the human sciences and with the problem of their method remains determinant even if the sphere of their methodology is overcome. Precisely insofar as it is conceived as ontological difference – or as the difference between Being and beings, between *Lichtung* or horizon and being-that-is-present – difference does not simply give rise to the repetition of eternally equal structures; rather, it is deployed as the divergence – ever historically qualified – between the de-terminative, *be-stimmend* horizon, or a given historical epoch and what is given as present within it.

But the drift of Being is also a drift in the second sense I have suggested, the direction in which Dasein drifts as it is drawn along and dispossessed, a process which makes the entire context of existence – as a context of meanings, as a concatenation of founding and founded – depend on a basic discontinuity. Dasein is in fact constituted as a whole on the basis of an anticipatory resolve with respect to death, in other words on the basis of a relationship with its own annihilation. In this way hermeneutical thinking, whether as a reflection on the question of interpretation or as an actual exercise in the reconstruction of historical/cultural horizons, is ultimately exposed to a condition of ungrounding. However, not only is the totality of meaning as constructed by hermeneutics *ultimately* dependent on this ungrounding condition, which suspends it in its definition. Also within the ambit of hermeneutics as a pure effort of *Erörterung* – i.e. as primarily an effort to integrate presence within the horizon of making-present – we can already see an instance of ungrounding which suspends the completion of the *recollection du sens* (to use Ricoeur's term), setting Dasein adrift in a drift that can neither be embraced nor mastered. Even purely on the level of the reconstruction of meaning or the integration of the present within that horizon of past and future which offers it forth, there is something that resists and makes integration impossible, and that is *the other*, the other Dasein who always sets his or her mark on the 'elements' – the meanings, works, events or institutions which one tries to integrate within the horizon.

Although in *Truth and Method* Gadamer does not say much about ontological difference (a fact which is in itself worth pondering), the centrality for Gadamerian hermeneutics of dialogue testifies to the persistence there of this fundamental element of Heidegger's thought. It is the presence of a plurality of Daseins that makes it impossible to conceive of the hermeneutical integration of the horizon of presence as a dialectical *Aufhebung*. The resistance of the other to integration, which means that the *Horizontverschmelzung* is always only provisional, is by no means a historical accident that has to be justified and explained on the basis of the ideal of a fundamentally integrated society (as Habermas views it in his discussion of Gadamer's hermeneutic in *On the Logic of the Social Sciences*).[16] Rather, Schleiermacher[17] was right to point out that *Missverstehen* is the natural condition with which all interpretation begins; at the same time, in a certain sense at least, it is also interpretation's destination, to the extent that the other never allows himself or herself to be absorbed within the horizon of the interpreter. A better way of putting this is to say that the fusion of horizons takes place to the extent to which each of the interlocutors 'renounces' his *own* horizon, not by renouncing the fact of having a horizon, but by renouncing the fact of managing it as his own or disposing of it as he pleases. This phenomenon of permanent 'renunciation' is attested by the modes in which the integration of individual horizons into anonymous suprapersonal horizons (which in turn also stand at the basis of the constitution of individual horizons) actually takes place in society. Gadamer aptly describes these modes in terms of the concept of *play*, emphasizing its *expropriating* dimensions. All social communication is a locus for the unfolding of ontological difference, to the extent that communication realizes that twofold game of integration and ungrounding, the game of *Anwesen* and *Anwesen-lassen*, the game to which *Andenken* pays attention, and only thus sets out to think Being authentically again.

This nexus between ontological difference, social dialogue and ungrounding no doubt needs further elaboration; but I think we can already say that Heideggerian ontological difference may be the difference which can indicate a way towards radical rethinking of hermeneutics, allowing it to become an 'ontological' theory of social communication. I am thinking in particular here of the steps taken in this direction by Karl Otto Apel, for whom the concept of communication is central, and also of more recent attempts to integrate the idea of difference into a philosophy of communication using systems theory, for example, in Wilden's *System and Structure*.[18]

153

But today Heidegger's idea of ontological difference, when read with an eye to its original intentions and implications, suggests yet another avenue for thought. I have already remarked that there is a second and more fundamental sense in which ontological difference seems to signify an ungrounding, rather than an integration, of the horizon of presence, and that is in its connection with being-towards-death. Difference is what originally distinguishes *Anwesenlassen*, the temporally articulated horizon, from being-that-is-present. Dasein only manages to locate present being within a horizon and to free itself from the domination of pure presence, to the extent that it is constituted as a historical continuity endowed with meaning; and this in virtue of a resolute anticipation of its own death. As a possibility that is authentic (and as authentic possibility), this makes the other possibilities of Dasein able to be ordered within a context. But although it functions primarily in this way, constituting the historicity of Dasein as a *continuum*, and hence as an *Andenken* that recollects the difference between *Anwesen* and *Anwesenlassen*, being-towards-death also shows that the historical continuity of Dasein is undermined by a discontinuity, for this continuity is founded on the (possible) annihilation of Dasein.

There are some allusions to this ungrounding dimension of death in the last part of *Der Satz vom Grund*, where the *losende Bindung*, the liberating bond that binds us to the tradition of thought, or the integration of the present into the hermeneutical horizon that governs it, is invoked to 'justify' the leap, which, based on the Heraclitan image of the *aion* as a playful divine child, seeks to think the nexus between Being and *Grund*, Being and *Ab-Grund*, by reference to the *game* into which we 'are brought as mortals, as those who are only to the extent that we dwell in proximity to death . . .' (SVG p. 186). Although I cannot linger here to make a detailed analysis of this passage from *Der Satz vom Grund*, it does seem to me that we can view it as affirming the presence

154

of another more primordial call within the call of the principle of reason and within its appeal to construct the texture of experience as a grounded concatenation; this is a call to recognize the whole context as depending on an 'ab-gründlich' or bottomless condition. The *aion* is a playful child, but we cor-respond to this call of the *Ab-grund*, of abysmal play, only insofar as we are mortal. The anticipatory resolve with respect to death which in *Being and Time* functions so as to constitute existence as a historical continuity, also functions to hang the continuity of existence on abysmal play. There is a question that has to be asked if we are to begin to pursue – in addition to the radicalization of hermeneutics in a general theory of communication and of generalized communication – this second avenue that seems to be opened up for thinking today by ontological difference. The question is: does Heideggerian being-towards-death necessarily have to be read in a rigorously ontological key, without any relationship to the *ontic* reality of dying or to the natural, biological and animal dimensions of Dasein as a living being? There is a danger that we may get lost in the play of difference/repetition in which the 'philosophy of difference' has got lost. Does not the ungrounding of the context of existence in the direction of an *Ab-grund* have to mean that the continuity of the historical/hermeneutical context of existing must be founded/ungrounded on a naturalness, an animality, or maybe even a silence that is more than the silence between words which makes possible the differential play of the signifier? This is the real *animal silence* which is the pro-venance of human words and to which, in some as yet still-to-be-discovered sense, these words refer.

At one and the same time then, we need a development of ontological difference in the direction of a general theory of communication, supported by contributions from psychology, information theory, studies on the pragmatics of communication and systems theory. We also need a reappraisal of ontological difference in terms of a stress on nature as the natural basis/background/ungrounding of culture. In developing as a theory of generalized communication, hermeneutics has already come into contact with genetics, biology and ethology. If these openings are to be founded from the point of view of difference, they will require a patient rereading of the Heideggerian idea of being-towards-death as it evolves from *Being and Time* to the later works. Only then will we be able to say whether it is meaningful from a Heideggerian viewpoint to take being-towards–death as indicating a biological/natural foundation for culture. Whatever the results of such a reappraisal, this does seem to be the direction in which ontological difference can still constitute a possible adventure for thought.

Notes

1   Now in *Margins of Philosophy*.
2   Cf. *Margins of Philosophy*, p. 27. The Heidegger reference is to 'The Anaximander Fragment' in M. Heidegger, *Early Greek Thinking*, trans. D. F. Krell and F. A. Capuzzi, New York/Evanston/San Francisco/London, 1975, p. 52.
3   *Margins of Philosophy*, p. 27.
4   Ibid., p. 7.
5   Ibid., p. 26.
6   Ibid., p. 23.
7   For example in studies like the one by S. Kofman, *Nietzsche et le métaphore*; on this, see my 'Nietzsche heute?' in *Philosophische Rundschau*, 1977, pp. 67–91.
8   Cf. *Writing and Difference*, p. 28.
9   G. Deleuze, *Différence et Répétition*, Paris, 1968, p. 92.
10 *Anti-Oedipus: Capitalism and Schizophrenia*, by G. Deleuze and F. Guattari, trans. R. Hurley, M. Seem and H. R. Lane, New York, 1977 and London, 1984.
11 Cf. *Anti-Oedipus*, p. 83.

12   On this topic see G. Deleuze, *Nietzsche and Philosophy*, trans. H. Tomlinson, London, 1983; and my introduction to the Italian translation, *Nietzsche e la filosofia*, trans. S. Tassinari, Florence, 1978.

13   Cf. *Thus spoke Zarathustra*, part III, 'The Covenant'.

14   *Truth and Method*, pp. 215ff.

15   This word has been employed to render the Italian term 'senso', which means both 'meaning/sense' and also 'direction'. (Translator's note.)

16   Cf. J. Habermas, *On the Logic of the Social Sciences*, Cambridge, 1988, pp. 143ff.

17   Cf. F. D. E. Schleiermacher, *Hermeneutics: the handwritten manuscripts*, ed. H. Kummerle, trans. J. Duke and J. Forstman, Missoula, Montana, 1977, p. 110.

18   A. Wilden, *System and Structure*, London, 1972.

7

Dialectic and Difference

AN area of Heidegger's thought where there is always fresh scope for reflection is the relation between *An-denken* and *Ge-Stell*. The first of these terms, *An-denken*, designates recollective thinking, the thinking that must put itself in a condition other than that of the metaphysical forgetting of Being. The second term, which I have elsewhere suggested rendering as im–position, is the term Heidegger uses to describe the 'constellation' in which modern man finds himself at the close of the epoch of metaphysics and at the moment of the triumph of technology. The *Ge-Stell* is the 'totality' of *Stellen*, that is of all that 'positing' which Heidegger views as making up the technical world; the condition in which man is challenged to push being into ever new 'uses' (QT p. 15) in a general imposition of calculation and planning which, in many of its aspects, is reminiscent of the 'totally administered' world of Adorno and the Frankfurt School. The problem about the relation of *An-denken* with *Ge-Stell* is that these terms are opposite and contradictory; there is no validity for Heidegger in the thesis 'away from *Ge-Stell* towards *An-denken*', which would have him thinking nostalgically of a world of 'authentic' relationships over against the levelling and de–historicization brought about by technology. On the contrary, again and again in his writings, another message is heard beyond and above that of the passages that seem to belong to the traditional critique of technology as 'alienation'. In this other message there is a 'positive' evaluation of technology in the context of over-coming metaphysics, but in the direction of *An-denken*, which excludes the possibility that overcoming metaphysics may be accomplished as the eradication of all recollection, or as the pure adequation of man to the 'challenge' of the technical de-historicization of the world. This Heideggerian stance is highly 'relevant', if that is a criterion we want to use. It is closely linked to the most stimulating and vital features of a current in twentieth-century thought that runs from Simmel to Bloch and Benjamin. What is more radical and problematic in Heidegger is precisely his insistence on the *recollective* dimension of *An-denken*, which always seems to be trying to bend the essence of technology in a direction that is foreign to it. There is in Heidegger the same accep-tance of the technical world as a human destiny that we find in Bloch and Benjamin. However, for Heidegger this des-tiny does not push man towards a condition that is totally rootless with respect to the humanistic tradition; rather, in Heidegger's view, man becomes a sort of *flâneur* whose essence is in a sense the (ironic, 'perverted') repetition of the humanistic experience. Not, therefore, 'away from *Ge-Stell* towards *An-denken*', but 'to *An-denken* in and through *Ge-Stell*'.

Are we then talking about a mechanism of dialectical reversal? If the name of Hegel comes to mind immediately, it is not simply because this process of going beyond metaphy-sics has a dialectical look to it,[1] apparently involving a reversal and possible reconciliation of opposites; it is also because one of the two opposed terms, the one that seems to constitute access to a post-metaphysical thought, is defined by reference to *recollection*. But it is exactly by explaining how and why recollection in Heidegger's post-metaphysical thought is not the same as what we find in Hegel's philoso-

159

phy that we shall explain how and why the passage from *Ge-Stell* to *An-denken* is not a reversal or dialectical *Aufhebung*. (The connection between the discourse about *Ge-Stell* and the *Auseinandersetzung* with Hegel is clearly visible in the two essays by Heidegger that comprise the volume entitled *Identity and Difference*. This might equally well be entitled 'Dialectic and Difference', since it is precisely in the Hegelian dialectic that the history of the notion of identity in the metaphysical tradition is in fact accomplished.)

In Hegel, thinking is deployed as memory because in his conception the truth of self-consciousness, expounded for the first time in modern philosophy by Descartes, becomes a process of the interiorization of exteriority articulated in time. This does not, however, mean that the nexus between the *speculativeness* of thinking (knowledge as knowledge of itself) and the *historicity* of thinking is truly clarified and 'founded'. There remains still a mystery about *why* Hegelian speculativeness must be identified with the historicity of knowledge. But this is the same problem as that of onto-theo-logy, the term Heidegger uses to describe the development of metaphysics – a theory of Being as Being – in its general structures, for example, that of substance – and at the same time a theory of the supreme Being on which all other beings depend. Both the relation between speculativeness and historicity in Hegel and the double configuration of metaphysics as ontology and theology are connections that metaphysics experiences without problematizing them authentically in terms of their common root. To get back to this root is equivalent to putting metaphysics itself into question, and, at least in a certain sense, taking leave of it. Even if we fail to give a full account of the connection (and to give such an account would in any case be to remain within the sphere of 'foundational' thinking and therefore of metaphysics), the fact remains that in Hegel *thinking is memory because knowledge is knowledge of itself*; the recollection at work in Hegel's *Phenomenology of the Spirit* is thus deeply marked by speculativeness. What dominates in this speculation is *appropriation*.

The consciousness that follows the phenomenological itinerary does not 'give itself up to' memory, but progressively appropriates what it has lived and what had remained, at least partially alien to it. In Hegel *Er-innerung* (remembrance, memory) is understood etymologically as *er-innern*, interiorization, the bringing within the subject of that which is initially given to him as external to him. Before this recollection (which Hegel more properly calls *Gedächtnis*) *Er-innerung* is a depositing of something in the reservoir of memory, memorization; and this means stripping the datum of experience (initially at least) of its particular and accidental character by turning it into a term in the history of the subject, and thus inserting it into a more universal context.[2] The double meaning of *Er-innerung* in Hegel – both recollection and memorization/interiorization – suggests that for him what is involved is a process of appropriation organized in a rigidly teleological fashion. The initial appropriation that takes place with the interiorization of the datum is only a step on the path towards a more complete appropriation, one that is accomplished by *Gedächtnis* as well as by imagination. In the Hegelian concept and practice of thinking, speculativeness, historicity and the teleological order of the process are necessarily linked together: 'For Hegel, the matter (*Sache*) of thinking is: Being, as thinking that thinks itself; and thinking comes to itself only in the process of its speculative development, thus running through stages of the variously developed, and hence of necessity previously underdeveloped, forms' (ID p. 45).

Forgetting and memory are inextricably bound up together in this Hegelian mode of conceiving and practising thinking. Perhaps one of the first authors to begin to throw light on this nexus was Nietzsche in the second part of his *Untimely Meditations*, and it is to this too that he owes his position as both the final thinker of metaphysics and the first thinker of 'what comes after'. This nexus is important because it does not concern Hegel alone, but the whole metaphysical tradition that reaches its culmination in him. It seems in Hegel as if metaphysics, which in Heidegger's view runs through the whole history of Western thought from Plato to Nietzsche, is not solely characterized by forgetting (of Being in favour of beings) but at the same time and in parallel by memory as *Er-innerung*, appropriation. Metaphysics is the thinking that corresponds to an epoch in which Being is given to man within the horizon of a *Grund*, of a foundation, or to use the original Greek term, of *logos*. There is no reason (*Grund*) for this event. From *Being and Time* onwards, Heidegger acknowledged in all his philosophical work that the domination of the idea of foundation is an essentially historical/cultural fact, ultimately because Being does not have extratemporal structures, for each of the ways it has of giving itself is a *Prägung*, an 'imprint' that is different every time. This means that we shall not be able to explain the way Being gives itself as foundation either: it is given/*es gibt* in this light, it happens according to this imprint, and that is all. If we recognize the historical/destinal[3] character of the self-giving of Being as foundation, i.e. that it is not historically 'explicable' on the basis of 'what came before', and of necessary consequences, we are thus also already at the margins of this *Prägung*, we are at the moment of a possible overcoming of metaphysics *and all this without being able to point to a foundation for our position.*

Here it becomes clear how close and yet diametrically opposed to one another are Hegel and Heidegger. For Hegel, the absolute self-consciousness of the spirit at the conclusion of the phenomenological itinerary is a 'logical' consequence of the process of the real/rational. It overcomes but does not deny this process. It accomplishes and concludes it in the sense that it totally interiorizes it, thereby being imprinted by it in its own structure. Absolute thought is the final product of real causations unfolded in history, of *logos* as efficient foundation/cause; it is also the *consciousness* deployed in the connections and the necessity of this process. For Hegel, the absolute position attained by consciousness is a *fact* (that which is real is rational), but a fact defined as the perfect realization of the rational. We can 'think' because we find ourselves at a certain point in history; but this constitutes no element of unfoundedness for thinking, because the point in history that we occupy is characterized as the perfect coincidence of real foundation (causation) and rational explanation.

For Heidegger too we are able to think because we find ourselves in a certain historical situation. But our situation – characterized by the fact that we begin to grasp the *Prägung* of Being as *logos* insofar as it too is *Prägung*, a historical/destinal imprint and no longer a 'necessary' structure – is also devoid of logic; it has no foundation and cannot have one.

In what sense does the process culminating in Hegel represent a determinate nexus of forgetting and memory? Heidegger calls metaphysics forgetting inasmuch as such thought has forgotten Being in favour of beings (and he has in mind the whole of Western thought since Plato, unfolding as a general theory of Being, onto-logia, and as a theory of the supreme Being, theo-logia). The dual configuration of metaphysics – as ontology and theology – is the fruit and expression of the forgetting in which it lives. The question about Being ('What is Being?') has from the start transformed itself into a question about the Being on which all others depend; however, it is by no means obvious that Being, which 'lets' beings be, can be identified purely and simply with that Being which causes them existentially. To have taken this as given is the mark of metaphysics, the *Prägung* of Being in the light of *Grund* or foundation. Once this identification of Being with foundation has been made, Being as different from beings has been forgotten, and the way is open for the need for recollection as a return from what is to what causes it, to the *Grund*, a process that is not a return *in infinitum* but ends with the 'supreme' Being, God. Metaphysical *recollection* is opened as such precisely by the *forgetting* of Being in its difference from beings.

Heideggerian *An-denken* involves a relation between forgetting and recollection too, but it is other than the one that prevails in the metaphysical tradition and culminates in Hegel. If we are to understand this we must have a general understanding of how and why thinking moves away from Hegel in the dialogue initiated by Heidegger with him, especially in *Identity and Difference*. Actually it is not a question of why and how, only of how, for where the logic of *Grund* is put into question, the 'why' can no longer be articulated. There is no foundation, no 'why' to our moving away from the thought of Hegel and metaphysics; what we know is that it is happening or rather that it has already happened. It is a fact like 'the death of God' as affirmed by Nietzsche. In Nietzsche the statement 'God is dead' has a much more literal meaning than is often believed. It is not the metaphysical proposition that God 'does not exist', since this would still imply a claim to be referring to some stable structure of reality, some order of Being, that is, the real 'existing' of God in the history of thought. Rather, it is the recognition of a happening, the happening in which Being no longer needs to be thought of as endowed with stable structures and ultimately with a foundation. This analogy is not one I want to pursue here; suffice it to say that Heidegger would not have accepted it as such, at least to the extent that for him Nietzsche belonged to the history of metaphysics, which recollective thought had to overcome. But strictly speaking, insofar as the statement 'God is dead' indicates the end of the logic of the foundation which dominates metaphysics, it is one proposition among others capable of legitimating the claim that Nietzsche is at one and the same time still a metaphysical thinker and a thinker who already announces 'what comes after'. To Heidegger it is the metaphysical thinker who comes out on top; Nietzsche's message is still a foundational one, for it says that with the death of God everything is 'brought back' to man. But this can be

164

read and interpreted in a more radically post-metaphysical fashion than Heidegger does. The 'eventual' character of Nietzsche's death of God, as of the call of *An-denken* in Heidegger, does not mean that it is fortuitous or inessential. Though what happens is neither necessary nor required by some pre-established logic of history, once it has happened it is our *Geschick*, it is that which is sent or destined for us, as a call to which we must respond in some way, and which we cannot ignore.

Heidegger alludes to this in *Identity and Difference*, when he talks about the freedom we have to think difference or not (which is equivalent, at least initially, to going beyond metaphysics or not). 'Our thinking is free either to pass over difference without a thought or to think of it specifically as such. But this freedom does not apply in every case. Unexpectedly it may happen that thinking finds itself called upon to ask: what does it say, this Being that is mentioned so often?' (ID p. 63). There is no stable structure of Being which is identifiable with difference and which thought is free either to look at or to look away from. As Heidegger began to show with his lecture on 'The essence of truth' in 1930, freedom is more originative than pure spiritual movement with regard to the stability of structures; freedom concerns the giving of these structures themselves, the opening of horizons in which are situated the alternatives with respect to which humans can then decide one way or another. Thus Heidegger's statement is to be read as follows: with regard to thinking or not thinking difference there may still be freedom for thought in 'psychological' terms, but this freedom is secondary in respect of a more essential event, that is, the fact of whether (in any case and independently of our decision) the call of difference resounds or not. Difference is not a structure of Being within which man's thought moves arbitrarily, turning to it or looking away from it, so we cannot describe it or talk about it at all except with reference to the *case* in which thought may be called on to

pay attention to it. We cannot speak of difference, i.e. begin
to overcome metaphysics, unless we describe the conditions
in which this case occurs which calls us in a peremptory
fashion.

Ge-Stell is just such a case, such a 'chance'. What tells us
that Hegel's position is not tenable (any more) is not some
illogicality internal to it; we do not get out of Hegel, or any
other thinkers, by means of a dialectical overcoming of
contradictions. (This may, incidentally, explain why Heidegger's descriptions of philosophies of the past are so often
'apologetic', carefully presenting each individual philosophy
as a connected whole that is in some sense necessary.) All
that we can have with the past is a *Gespräch*, a dialogue, and
that arises to the extent that we start from different positions.
'Position' is to be understood primarily in a literal sense, as
Heidegger demonstrates by tracing *Er-örterung* (discussion,
explanation) to its etymological root, *Ort*, place, which
means that the term may also be translated as 'collocation'.[4]
It is the historical/cultural (or more properly historical/
destinal, in Heideggerian language) place where *we are* and
from where we speak in our dialogue with the past. The
most important thing in the idea of dialogue is this stress on
the otherness of our *Ort* in relation to that of our interlocutor. But is not our *Ort* also and importantly co-
determined by the fact that Hegel existed and put forward
certain theses? This question has received prolonged elaboration by hermeneutics since Dilthey, in recent times chiefly
under the inspiration of Heidegger. But to take for granted
that the *Ort* in which we are situated as interpreters is always
co-determined by the historical/cultural *Wirkung* of the
interlocutor with whom we engage in dialogue, involves an
uncritical acceptance of the historicist image of the *continuity*
of historical becoming. In fact historicism, whether in the
Hegelian metaphysical formulation or in the Diltheyan version, seems in essence diametrically opposed to hermeneutics, inasmuch as it is dominated by the model of continuity.

This is quite clear in Hegelian historicism, whose most coherent outcome from this point of view seems to be Gentilian *attualismo*. But what remains to be seen is the extent to which Dilthey's vitalistic conclusions, and even more so those of his followers and interpreters, again merely reveal the predominance of the model of continuity, which makes hermeneutics meaningless. If we follow the Hegelian philosophy of the spirit in basing continuity on history, hermeneutics loses all meaning because the only thing that deserves to survive is what is in fact already present in the successive stages of the development of the spirit, and so to read and interpret the past is merely to become conscious of what one always already is. On the other hand, if like Dilthey we refer continuity back to life, then hermeneutics still makes no sense because what we find at the bottom of everything is not the ever-different 'contents' of lived experience, but the structures of this experience, which remain everywhere the same.

This is the dilemma Heidegger tries to evade when he tries to develop the distinction between *das Selbe* and *das Gleiche*, the Same and the Equal. He is well aware that there can be no *Gespräch* with the tradition of thought, nor can there even be history without some *Durchgängiges*, something permanent that runs through the various epochs of Being, and therefore also the various moments of disclosure and *Prägungen* of the truth of Being. But this *Durchgängiges* cannot ever be something equal understood as a generality or *telos* that the various moments combine to prepare for. Instead it is to be thought as a 'Same'. The *Selbe* that traverses history is the fact that history signifies *Ueberlieferung* or trans-mission of messages, *Gespräch* in which every word is always already *Ent-sprechung* or a response to an *Anspruch*, to a call which as such always also transcends the person who receives it. It is only with reference to this idea of the Same that in Heidegger's view we can talk of history. For him it is not the history of things (such as works, individual existence, or forms, with their concatenations in the events of coming to birth and dying), nor is it an evolution towards a *telos*, nor a mere return of the equal. Rather, it is a history of messages, in which *the response never exhausts the call*, precisely because in some way the response actually depends on the call. And yet, the full implications of this hermeneutical model of history have never yet been spelt out properly, either by Heidegger himself or by his interpreters and followers.[5] However, we can say that in history as a transmission of messages, the Same is the unthought that presents itself in each proposition as reserve, as that residuum of transcendence conserved by a proposition in every response, and it is to this 'unsaid', this 'unthought', that the dialogue with the past relates, which inasmuch as it is unthought, is never past but also always yet to come. The Same understood in this sense is what historical diversity or *Verschiedenheit* allows to appear (cf. ID p. 45). With respect to the Equal, whether as universal structure or as unifying *telos*, there cannot arise truly diverse historical positions, but only eventually a greater or lesser coincidence with the universal or different steps along a single path of development. Only if there is a Same as unsaid can there be truly different dislocations of the interlocutors of history as *Ueberlieferung*. More plainly we might say that there is diversity in history only if there is a Same that cannot be consumed in the Equal, *that is*, a Same that remains not-said and not-thought but yet always the Same, for otherwise differences could not even appear as such, and there would be neither *Gespräch* nor *Ueberlieferung*. But the being of the Same, precisely to the extent that it remains unsaid, can be 'proved' only by the very fact of transmission.

Our dis-location with respect to Hegel and the history of metaphysics is defined by the term *Ge-Stell*. (When Heidegger uses the word 'our' he is alluding to the historical/destinal constellation into which we his contemporaries are thrown, and with respect to which his discourse claims to apply.) In German the word *Ge-Stell* currently has the meaning of 'pedestal, shelves, framework', but Heidegger treats it as a composite of *Ge* and *Stell*, by analogy with words like *Ge-birg*, in which the prefix *Ge* placed before *Birg*, *Berg* (mountain) has the idea of 'together', so that *Ge-birg* is a range of mountains. *Ge-Stell* is the ensemble of *stellen* or 'setting in place'. The technical world is the world in which Being is *set in place*. All that is, in this world, is related to *stellen*, a verb with which Heidegger associates the numerous meanings of its German compounds; thus, for example, in the technical world, in addition to 'setting in place', what dominates is also producing (*her-stellen*), representing (*vor-stellen*), ordering (*be-stellen*), pursuing (*nach-stellen*) and consulting (*stellen*, in one of its colloquial senses) (cf. QT pp. 14–15 and note).

An English version of *Ge-Stell* might be *im-position*, in which the hyphen indicates a particular 'etymological' use of the term, and there is an echo of the 'setting in place' suggested by the German *stellen*, at the same time as the general sense of an 'urging' that we cannot escape, something which Heidegger conveys by the way he employs the word. The technical world described as *Ge-Stell* is the world of planned production, served by knowledge as representation, and in which man is repeatedly interpellated in an ordering process imposing on him a continuous pursuit of things to serve as reserves or resources, and these serve the ever-increasing development of production. Heidegger also uses the term *Heraus-forderung* to describe the totality of this activity, an expression we may render as *pro-vocation*. In the world of *Ge-Stell*, man and Being relate to one another in the mode of reciprocal pro-vocation. The being of beings is related to man as something ever to be manipulated, man provokes beings to uses that are perpetually new and alien on the basis of their increasingly implausible 'nature'. Looked at from the angle of the reciprocal *Heraus-forderung* of man and Being, *Ge-Stell* emerges more clearly for what it is: not simply a determinate historical order of production and existence, but the *Er-eignis* of the Being in which we are by destiny located. Written as it often is by Heidegger with a hyphen, *Er-eignis* alludes to an event in which Being occurs as a game of 'appropriation', *eigen* meaning 'proper'. In *Ereignis* man is appropriated (*vereignet*) to Being, while Being is consigned (*zugeeignet*) to man (cf. ID pp. 31ff.). The reciprocal provocation in which Being and man are related in the im-position that characterizes the technical world is the event of the reciprocal trans-propriation of man and Being. It is incorrect to say that the *Ge-Stell* is a form of the *Ereignis*, as though the structure of the event of Being could be realized in different forms. The *Ereignis* is a *singulare tantum*, and Heidegger is constantly obliged to resist the tendency inherent in the language handed down by metaphysics, the only one we have, to conceive the Being-beings relation in terms of universal and particular. The *Ereignis* is unique: it is the reciprocal trans-propriation of man and Being, and this transpropriation happens in *Ge-Stell* and nowhere else. If this is so, *Ge-Stell* is also the condition – as yet not explicitly recognized – out of which Heidegger speaks in *Being and Time*; in other words, already the starting-point for Heidegger the phenomenologist who raises his initial question about Being. In fact we are able to raise the question about Being and escape from metaphysical forgetting only because and to the extent to which Being occurs in the form of transpropriation, in other words in the form of the *Ge-Stell*. Nor could we even think of Being as *Ereignis* if we were not interpellated by *Ge-Stell*. The history of metaphysics is the history of the forgetting of Being in its difference from beings, thus of Being as *Ereignis*; but it appears to be so *only* when looked at from the dis-location in which *Ge-Stell* locates us. If on one hand *Ge-Stell* brings to accomplishment metaphysics as the meditation of *Grund* (and in the technical world everything is a regulated concatenation of cause and effect where *Grund* always triumphs), on the other it also finally makes Being appear no longer the foundation to which man refers but rather the occurring of the reciprocal transpropriation of man and Being. In the technical world Being as foundation disappears; everything amounts to 'position', every foundation is founded in turn and man lives in the arc of this foundation. In the universal manipulation which involves man not simply as subject but also often as object (from the various forms of social domination through to genetic engineering), *Ereignis* is announced, and Being is freed (starting) from the imprint of *Grund*. It is the *Ge-stell* that opens us to grasp the *difference* which, by remaining unthought, has always dominated the metaphysical tradition (most recently masked as Hegelian dialectic). For all its perpetual talk of Being and beings, metaphysics has still persistently forgotten that one constantly leads back to the other in a game that never lets itself be stopped. If we ask what Being is, the answer comes: Being is what beings are, it is the Being of beings, while beings in their turn are to be defined only as the beings of Being, those beings that have Being, that are. What is clear in this circle, is 'that when we deal with the Being of beings and with the beings of Being, we deal in each case with difference. Thus we think of Being rigorously (*sachlich*) when we think of it in its difference with beings, and of beings in their difference with Being' (ID p. 62). To think Being and beings constantly in their difference, and not to follow the foundational thought of metaphysics which reduces one to the other, means to discover both as *transitive*. Being is what a being is (as complement). A being is what Being is (its complement). 'The "is" here speaks transitively, in transition (*übergehend*). Being here becomes (*west*) present in the manner of a transition to beings' (ID p. 64).

For beings, to be does not chiefly mean to consist and subsist in a defined space-time; if anything, it means to exist in the ecstatic sense that *Being and Time* recognizes as essential to man's existence. Things are inasmuch as they

171

come to being or occur; and their occurring is a being – inserted into a process of appropriation-expropriation, in which Being makes them happen and at the same time continuously ex-terminates[6] them, illimits them and de-stitutes them. In their difference beings and Being are related just as *Ankunft* (the advent of the being) is related to *Ueberkommnis* (the coming-over of Being over the being) (cf. ID p. 64).

If we are to understand the nexus between *Ge-Stell* and *Ereignis*, and thus understand why that culmination of the metaphysical forgetting of Being in technology can at the same time be the first step of *An-denken*, we need first of all to bear in mind this transitive aspect of Being as affirmed in *Ereignis*; and we need to refer it (without reducing it) to *Herausforderung*, the provocation that constitutes the world of technological im-position. From this point of view there is at least some justification in the complaint that Heidegger still belongs to the history of nihilism, namely, to the thought which assumes Being to be producible, manipul-able, and transformable, and consequently in principle also destructible and capable of being annihilated.[7] The nihilism peculiar to technology, which thinks Being (even if only initially) as occurring in a game of reciprocal transpropria-tion with man, is in fact the step that must be taken if we are to begin to listen to the call of *Ereignis* (outside which *there is* no stable unvarying Parmenidean Being). Only by listening to this call can we realize the possibility of freedom that is contained in *Ge-Stell*, though as yet still not actualized. *Ge-Stell* is not however all of *Ereignis* but only its 'prelude'.

What we experience in the frame of the constellation of Being and man through the modern world of technology is a *prelude* to what is called the event of appropriation. This event, however, does not necessarily persist in its prelude. For in the event of appropriation the possibility arises that it may overcome the mere dominance of the frame to turn it into a more original appropriating (ID pp. 36–7).

Ge-Stell initially shows the transitivity of Being; in this show-ing there is a possibility of liberation from the pure dominat-ion of im–position, which thought has yet to explore whether in theory or practice. The call for a 'return to Parmenides' in the name of a struggle against nihilistic technology offers to the eventuality of Being as shown in *Ge-Stell* (and emerging in philosophy with *Being and Time*) a pure and simple return to the *stability* of Being as theorized by the metaphysical tradi-tion. But this stability *is no longer given* anywhere, because in the meantime the metaphysical tradition has proceeded towards *Ge-Stell*; in other words, 'God is dead'.

What constitutes *Ge-Stell* as a prelude to *Ereignis* is its mobile and transitive character. Heidegger alludes to this by using terms such as *Reigen*, 'ring' (PLT p. 180) to describe the 'mirror game of the world' in which the transpropriating event of Being occurs. The most commonly stressed aspect of technology, as aspect regarded as almost demonic, is the governance of planning, calculation and potentially total organization. But in Heidegger's interpretation of *Ge-Stell* this is subordinate to an *urging* as continuous dislocation, as suggested by his use of the various compounds of *stellen* and his choice of the other term *Herausforderung*, provocation. The call of technique, in *Ge-Stell*, means that 'Our whole human existence everywhere sees itself challenged – now playfully and now urgently, now breathlessly and now ponderously – to devote itself to the planning and calculat-ing of everything', persisting with this planning 'past all bounds' (ID pp. 34–5). We could call all this the 'shaking' in which beings find themselves caught in *Ge-Stell*; and it is *this shaking* that makes *Ge-Stell* 'a first, oppressing flash of the Er-eignis' (ID p. 38).

That mobility is predominant in *Ge-Stell* is confirmed by other elements, especially the way a whole group of terms is used in these pages from *Identity and Difference*, in particular the whole discourse on *Schwingen* or oscillation. 'The event of appropriation [*Er-eignis*] is that realm, vibrating within itself, through which man and Being reach each other in their nature, achieve their active nature by losing those qualities with which metaphysics has endowed them' (ID p. 37). To think *Er-eignis* as such, it is necessary to work on the construction of its 'fluctuating' (*schwebend*) edifice, making use of the instrument of language. Oscillation, fluctuation and the shaking of provocation lead man and Being to lose their metaphysical determinants and so lead to the threshold of *Ereignis*. The determinants attributed to man and Being by metaphysics are variously illustrated in the occasional passages Heidegger devotes to the tracing of their history: in general, metaphysics thinks man and Being respectively as *subject* and *object*. In the parts of *Identity and Difference* I have been referring to, he seems rather to be thinking of the determinants that man and Being take on in the division (also metaphysical) between nature and history, according to the models of physics and historiography (cf. ID p. 40). For the thought of our century, man and Being are metaphysically determined in the opposition between nature and history that governs the distinction between *Naturwissenschaften* and *Geisteswissenschaften*, 'natural sciences' and 'human sciences', on one side the reign of necessity and general laws, on the other the reign of freedom and individuality. But these are the very distinctions that are lost in the 'round' of '*Ge-Stell*'. In the technical world where everything is an object of manipulation on man's part, man himself becomes universally manipulable in turn; but this is not merely a sign of some demoniacal character in technology, it is also and inseparably the shining of *Ereignis*, as the crisis and dissolution of the metaphysical determinants of man and Being. And in its turn the loss of metaphysical determinants, not now replaced by others, but merely with a view to collocation in a more originative 'domain' in which nature and history stand in a more plastic and transitive relation, is a further element that defines the mobility of *Ge-Stell*. Ideas like that of the *Sprung* (leap) and the *Schritt zurück* (step back) are linked to this mobility in *Identity and*

Difference: these are the features of recollective thinking, the thinking which prepares to respond to the call of *Ereignis*, and thus distinguishes itself from dialectical thinking and in general from metaphysical thinking as return to a *Grund*.

So far what has been to the fore in our view of *Ge-Stell* has been its provocative character which violently dis-locates man and Being from the positions assigned to them by metaphysics (reminiscent of the violence involved in the phenomenological discovery of truth in *Being and Time*). By dis-locating them in this way, it also locates them in the sphere of oscillation that is *Ereignis* as reciprocal transpropriation. How and why is this thinking, corresponding to the call of *Ge-Stell* as a prelude to *Ereignis*, to be designated as recollection? It is true that in losing metaphysical characteristics man is ready to relate to Being by thinking it in its *difference* from beings, but why call such a thought of difference *An-denken* or recollection? Definitely not in the sense that thought, dominated by *Ge-Stell*, represents difference to itself, bringing it out of the oblivion into which it had fallen. Difference may be grasped only in its transitivity, which is also its transitoriness.[8] Thus the thought that thinks difference is also always constituted by remembering, which means referring to that which is 'past': and this is because difference is always given primarily as deferring, as *Ankunft* and *Ueberkommnis*, the being's being-given in presence and the interference of the being that passes over it,[9] sweeps over it in a flux and also causes it to be continually passed by.[10] The as yet unthought nexus between Being as *Ereignis* and being-towards-death underlies the connection between difference as a distinction between Being and beings and difference as deferring or spacing in time. There is no thought of difference that is not recollection. This is not simply because difference is in fact forgotten by metaphysical thought, but also because difference is primarily deferring, it is in fact the very temporal articulation of experience which is essentially connected with the fact of our mortality.

But could it not still be said that *Ge-Stell* as the shaking-up of existence liberates us finally from any relation with the past and from the need to think by constant remembrance? The thinking which cor-responds to *Ereignis* and which is opened by *Ge-Stell* may in other words be equivalent to a thinking that, having taken leave of a metaphysics of foundational return, is therefore henceforth rid of all nostalgia, historical depth and memory. Heidegger's response to this is that *Ge-Stell* puts us in a position to take a 'step back' (*Schritt zurück*) with respect to the logic of foundations and (for that very reason) to see its history in its totality (ID p. 49). This step back is the same one that in the first essay in *Identity and Difference* Heidegger calls a 'leap', *Sprung*, thereby underlining its *discontinuity* in regard to the path taken by metaphysics. As such, this is in no way a return to the origins (ID p. 50). It is rather a distancing which is in contrast with Hegelian dialectical recollection; the latter is thought as the culmination of a process and so in substantial continuity with it. Though this may allow the appropriation of the process in its totality, it does not allow a grasping of it as a whole from an external point of view.

The experience of *Ge-Stell* leads us to grasp *Ereignis*, and therefore above all to uncover the eventual nature of Being, its being given under marks that are different every time. At bottom, oscillation is not identifiable with the mere coming and going of man as caught in technology and production, although it is linked to this world as one of its possibilities. Oscillation is the dis-covering (coming to light) of the eventuality of Being; the universal manipulability established by the technical world throws light retrospectively on the eventual nature of every epoch of the man-Being relation. This may be the difference – which Heidegger often stresses without ever really laying it to rest – between thinking technology and thinking the *essence* of technology, an essence which is itself not actually technical. A first attempt at clarifying this might be to suggest that the givenness of

beings as a manipulable totality in the horizon of provocation is not something that man controls, something he has
produced technically and can change by resorting to decidable and plannable procedures. More deeply, to think the
essence of technology as something non-technical signifies
seeing in *Ge-Stell* a cipher of *Ereignis*. To find in the
'reflection' on *Ge-Stell* only a generalization about the category of manipulability would mean to limit oneself to the
technicality of technology. We go beyond this if we grasp in
its depth what is alluded to by the provocation of *Ge-Stell*,
namely, the transitivity of Being, which dis-locates man
from his metaphysical position as subject, a position in
which, however, he remains when he affirms universal
manipulability. This may help us to understand how Heidegger thinks his own difference from Nietzsche. The
Nietzschean will to power seems to him to think technology
and not its essence; he sees it as an affirmation of manipulability but not yet as a turn to the transitivity of Being in
Ereignis. To start from *Ge-Stell* and accede to the totality of
the history of metaphysics in the sense of the *Schritt zurück*
and not in the sense of a Hegelian dialectical accomplishment, will mean then to turn to this totality not as a process
that is teleologically ordered and causally necessitated, but as
a *sphere of oscillation*; to attend above all to the multiplicity of
'drifts' that being has in the course of its history, without
being persuaded to order them in a system from within,
without the 'step back'. In his writings Heidegger developed
an analysis of the relation between the triumph of modern
technology and the triumph of historicist thought. What
these have in common is an *assurance* of the position of the
present (so both lie within the horizon of *stellen*) with respect
to nature and the historical past. To reconstruct historically
(historiographically) the roots of the situation in which we
find ourselves is actually equivalent to assuring ourselves of
it, in the same way that we assure ourselves of it by
dominating it technically.[11] However, just as there is a

177

post-metaphysical valency in technique, that is in *Ge-Stell* taken as a prelude to *Ereignis*, so must we expect there to be a possible post-metaphysical valency in *Historismus*, and it is to be sought in the oscillatory effect which, analogously with the shaking-up of metropolitan existence, is exercised by the recognition of the multiplicity of *Prägungen*, or marks impressed on the man-Being relation in history, the history represented by *Historie*.

The world of *Ge-Stell* is not solely the world of totally deployed technology, of provocation/production/assurance. It is also and inseparably the world of *Historie*, of historiography as the laborious reconstruction of the past, in which historiographical industry, by virtue of its own excess, eventually liquidates any sacral or hierarchical relations with this same past. The man of *Ge-Stell* is not ignorant of history but he has with the past the relation described by Nietzsche in the second of his *Untimely Meditations*, that of a kind of tourist wandering in the garden of history, history that has become a sort of 'natural park', or, in modern terms, a supermarket or even a theatrical costumier's studio. For Nietzsche, such a historiographical relation to history is, of course, the height of historical unproductiveness and lack of style. This, however, is probably true only for the early Nietzsche, for the increasing predominance in his subsequent work of the notion of the mask, as against any superstitious belief in truth, authenticity, or 'ownness', involves a re-evaluation of the phantasmagorical aspects of *Historismus*. The will to power is thus primarily the will to hide with the masks of all the costumes of history, without relation to any 'truth' supposedly hidden underneath them.

Heidegger's polemic against *Historismus* too does not ultimately aim at a restoration of an 'authentic' relation with the past. He does not see the dialogue with *Ueberlieferung* as tending to define the coordinates of the present in such a way as to assure oneself of it and fix it in its allegedly authentic condition; rather, the dialogue inaugurates a movement of

Ueberkommnis, an interference and engulfing in which the present is thrown into the oscillating abyss of *Ereignis*. It is here that we can see the difference between Heidegger and Hegel in respect of the problem of the memory/forgetting nexus. In Hegel memory has the function of a return to an unfolding of the *Grund*, it is *begründend* and *ergründend*, it founds and explains; but in Heidegger, the drift of memory is ungrounding. This is not *er-innern* in which the subject interiorizes what was external to it, consuming its alterity; it is rather an entering (of Dasein) into otherness. The process has no end, and its movement is the indefinite oscillation among *Prägungen*, the imprints in which the Being–man relation has historically been given. Heidegger is dismissive in his descriptions of the *ahistoricity* of the technical world and indeed the technical world in general, viewing it as the final culmination of the metaphysical forgetting of Being, but this ahistoricity, like all that constitutes *Ge-Stell*, is also related to the prelude to *Ereignis*, as a de-stitution of the historicist relationship with the past and a resonance of an (admittedly problematic) call of *Geschick*, of sending/destiny.

The failure to give full development to this aspect of *Ge-Stell* is a limitation of the Heideggerian discourse; but the way forward is clearly signposted by the definition of *Ge-Stell* as prelude to *Ereignis*. To go down this way is to begin to resolve the problem from which I began, the problem of the nexus between *Andenken* and *Ge-Stell*, not simply in a general way, highlighting how *Ge-Stell* itself is the starting-point for a recollection of difference, but in a further sense. This sense is more problematic in the letter of the Heideggerian text. I am thinking of the idea that *Ge-Stell*, in its characteristic a-historicity (the vertiginous static of technology as repetition or the 'production of a series'?) also gives *An-denken* its tonality as a recollection of the past *not* in being a return to a *Grund*, not in terms of an assurance of the coordinates of the present, but as an ungrounding and

179

de-stitution of present peremptoriness in the abyssal relation with *Ueberlieferung*.

Only thus can we understand how, in the two essays in *Identity and Difference*, Heidegger can associate *Ge-Stell* with the 'leap' and the 'step back' which always imply a relation with the past, an *Andenken* in the usual sense of the word. The reference to *Ge-Stell* and to the (potential) post-metaphysical bearing of technology serves, however, to give a decisive significance to the hermeneutical outcome of Heidegger's thought. The dialogue with *Ueberlieferung* is neither an effort to recover a constant universal element such as Being or truth, nor is it a return to a *Grund* and a deployment of its founding/appropriating force, as in the Hegelian dialectic. A connection must be made between the *Auseinandersetzung* Heidegger carries on with Hegel in both the essays in *Identity and Difference*, and his meditation on the technical world. Only the rooting of *An-denken* in *Ge-Stell* can exclude any nostalgic 'traditionalist' – or in any way metaphysical – reading of *An-denken*. Named and made possible by the call of *Ge-Stell*, the recollection to which we must entrust ourselves if we are to accede to a thinking no longer metaphysical, is an entering into the past, producing a dis-location, a sense of loss and an oscillation that removes from the present its cogency and peremptoriness.

The purely 'negative' dimension of this *Er-innerung* is neither provisional nor marginal; for Heidegger foundation can only be given as ungrounding. This is true in a variety of senses. The relation to the past in the form of a leap or step back or an oscillation means excluding the possibility of this relation attaining a fixed point. One leaps towards the sphere in which we always already are, but this sphere is precisely a domain of oscillation, distinguished by the fact that in it man and Being constantly lose the characteristics attributed to them by metaphysics. Not in order to acquire other charac-teristics, since that would make the oscillation only a provi-sional movement, susceptible of settling into a new state of stability, into some new *Geborgenheit*, intimacy, authenticity, or truth of the (substantive) essence of man. Oscillation is dialogue with *Ueberlieferung*, a dialogue that lets tradition be as such and carries it on, for ever remaining an intra-historical act.

This dialogue with *Ueberlieferung*, taken in its mobile sense as a game of calls and replies that are always historically and destinally limited, is the only way we can manage to depict a thought that does not aspire to be foundational in the metaphysical sense of the term and none the less is still thought. The *Durchgängiges* which, according to Heidegger, speaks through the various epochs of Being, is not an Equal but a Same, which makes differences be. The *Durchgängiges* is the actual difference that unfolds as the constitutive *finitude* of every historical horizon and is constituted as such only to the extent that it is a dialogue between these horizons. Difference is not revealed as something other, through and beyond the historical dialogue of finite perspectives; it is only that which allows finite perspectives and makes them be in their multiplicity that is always delimited, sent each time (*je und je geschicklich*).

What do we really experience in taking the leap, the step back, in the oscillation set in motion by *Ge-Stell* and unfolding in finite dialogue with *Ueberlieferung*? We are not experiencing some metaphysical unity or Equal; rather, we experience the Same, which is in fact only that in respect to which the individual historical/destinal *Prägungen* of the man-Being relation are constituted and destituted in their finitude, for ever in dialogue from transitory, momentary and ephemeral standpoints. To experience the Same is to experience historicity as *Geschicklichkeit*, the finite destinality of every historical/epochal situation. In the end this may seem to be yet another way of encountering being-towards-death, which seemed in the writings after *Being and Time* to have lost the central position it had earlier, without ever entirely disappearing from the horizon, but rather re-

emerging at decisive moments in a 'shining' and unarticu-
lated mode.[12]

The ahistoricity constitutive of *Ge-Stell*, understood not
only as a loss of roots, but also in its post-metaphysical
sense, as an aspect of the prelude to *Ereignis*, imprints the
recollection towards which *Ge-Stell* leads us in what may be
defined as a 'weak' or 'enfeebled' historicity or temporality.
We have here a very complex kind of game whose individual
movements are not all explicit in the Heideggerian text.
What is experienced in oscillation is difference understood as
das Selbe that makes historical/destinal differences be (ID
p. 45). Historical/destinal differences are the imprints which,
each time, form the outline of the man-Being relation to
which we respond, i.e. the historical finitude of Dasein
(man), which is not reducible either to a pure historicist
relativity (involving an absolutization of the course of history, even when it is rid of all necessity and all teleology)
nor to the flow of 'life' (itself thus absolutized as well). The
sphere of oscillation to which thought accedes by responding
to the call of *Ge-Stell* is a sphere in which metaphysical
characteristics, and in particular the nature/history distinction founded on the schemas of historiography and physics
(and in general of the modern natural sciences) are suspended. We experience this suspension, in a zone 'prior' to
the metaphysical rigidification of these two fields, if we
experience the historical/destinal finitude of existence in
relation to death, *not* as a means of access to something else
(to transcendence or to the stability of Being). Being,
existence, time, are here experienced essentially under the
sign of *decline*.[13] The name of the West, the *Abendland*, which
Heidegger interprets as the 'land of the twilight (of Being)'
here takes on a further sense, which is not purely 'negative'
either but rather a prelude to the *Ereignis*: The *Abendland* is
not simply the land where, with the unfolding of technology
as loss of roots and soil, Being collapses and dissolves in
accomplished nihilism, nor is it only the land where in the

end there is nothing left of Being as such, so that man is freed from metaphysical hindrances and can give himself over entirely to the total manipulation and organization of the world. It is also the destinal land where Being is given in the actual form of decline. This is not a fact to be deprecated amid lamentations for a lost fullness of authenticity, nor is it to be welcomed as a liberation from all nostalgia with a view to the unfolding of the will to power. All of this is certainly present *as well* in the destinal essence of the West, but as part of a vaster horizon, which, even on the historiographical level makes unsustainable any interpretation of Heidegger exclusively and rigidly in terms of one or other of these two readings of 'twilight'.

This vaster horizon is the one in which Being is experienced in terms of 'weak' temporality, in other words, not so much as the articulation of past, present and future in relation to a still-humanistic dimension of decision, as might seem to be implied by the most 'existentialistic' parts of *Being and Time*. Temporality is not only or primarily the self-constitution of historical (or existential) history in an organic context by virtue of an anticipatory resolve with respect to death. It is also and more radically de-stitution of all historical/hermeneutical continuity in relation to the very *fact* of death, experienced as that which makes every historical/cultural situation ephemeral, and experienced therefore as the place for the unfolding of that force of the Same which causes destinal differences between epochs and existences.

This leads me to suggest a new hypothesis about the significance of the *Kehre*, the 'change of direction' in Heidegger's thought[14] after *Being and Time*. I suspect that it may have been determined by an increasingly radical experience of the temporality of Being, an experience of Being *as* time, not, however, in the sense in which this connection was lived by existentialism and before that by the metaphysical tradition, where time was the time of decision, of the structuring articulation of the *ekstases*. Rather, Heidegger began to understand time as an endless passing, declining, ecstasy, in the sense of going outside oneself and entering another that remains for ever other. Moreover, Heidegger explicitly refers the idea of *Zeit*, time, to that of *Zeitigung*, maturation (of fruit, of the living).[15] Being is time inasmuch as it is maturation and growing old and so ephemerality.

It may perhaps seem that in the end we are left with nothing more than the identification of the experience of *An-denken* with a kind of 'wisdom' expressed by the Greek words *pathei mathos*. This leaves Heidegger's readers in some perplexity, especially in relation to the conclusions of contemporary hermeneutics, which is based on him.[16] Probably more consideration now needs to be given to the reasons for this perplexity; it is often bound up with the persistent aspiration to recover a 'strong' temporality as intrinsic to Being, for example, *An-denken* as a rediscovery of an 'authentic' relation with Being, and perhaps also as a non-'alienated' dimension of individual and social existence.

But even though it is unable to lead towards a sense of 'strong' time, *An-denken* cannot be just a resigned sanction of existence; rather, by the oscillation that characterizes it, it suspends and 'ungrounds' what exists in its claims to definitiveness and cogency, it takes shape as a truly critical thinking, preserved from the danger of indicating as present, at one time or another, *das Selbe* or authenticity. In addition, without ever expecting to come 'into the presence of' Being, *An-denken*, to the extent that it refers to *Zeit* as *Zeitigung*, sets out on the way towards thinking Being as temporality, as living life (and therefore also as passion, *eros*, need and welcome), as growing old and decline. In such a way it includes in Being, as the essential way it is given, all those features excluded from it by the metaphysical tradition in its quest for assurance and so for force (and the violence bound up with the imposition of presence). Thus too is continued the work begun by Heidegger when he first announced the programme summed up in the title *Being and Time*.

Notes

1 Heidegger speaks of an 'overcoming' (*Ueberwindung*) of meta-physics in EP pp. 84ff., but in the same place he interprets *Ueberwindung* as *Verwindung*, 'getting over' metaphysics (but also starting it up again) with a range of resonances that exclude any possibility of a dialectical reading.

2 The meaning of *Erinnerung* in Hegel has been the subject of a very fine study by Valerio Verra ('Storia e memoria in Hegel', in the volume edited by F. Tessitore, *Incidenza di Hegel*, Naples, 1970, pp. 339–65); the reader is referred to this for a fuller defence of my treatment of Hegel.

3 This is my rendering of the Heideggerian term *geschicklich*, which constantly recurs in the later works, along with *Geschick*, from which it is derived as its adjectival or adverbial form. *Geschick* is understood by Heidegger as 'destiny, transmission'; but he also plays on its assonance with *Ge-schichte* (history) and *geschichtlich* (historical). For clarification of these concepts, and of similar ones in the volume, the reader is referred to my books *Essere, storia, e linguaggio in Heidegger*, Turin, 1963, and *Introduzione a Heidegger*, Bari, 1971.

4 On this topic cf. *Essere, storia e linguaggio in Heidegger*, p. 153, and the passages cited and discussed there.

5 See esp. H. G. Gadamer, *Truth and Method*, and K. O. Apel, *Towards a Transformation of Philosophy*.

6 This term was suggested in the course of a seminar discussion by U. Galimberti; see his *Linguaggio e civiltà*, Milan, 1977.

7 This is E. Severino's thesis in *L'essenza del nichilismo*, Brescia, 1972; *Gli abitatori del tempo*, Rome, 1978; *Techne. Le radici della violenza*, Milan, 1979.

8 On this topic see my essay on *An-denken* above.

9 Italian 'che lo tra-passa'.

10 Italian 'lo fa continuamente trapassare'.

11 Cf. again *Essere storia e linguaggio*, ch. 1, and esp. pp. 25ff.

12 On the question of death and its development in Heidegger's thought, one of the most useful and penetrating works is by Ugo M. Ugazio, *Il problema della morte nella filosofia di Heidegger*, Milan, 1976.

13 J. Beaufret also discusses 'decline', I believe in a more limited sense; see his *Dialogue avec Heidegger*, Paris, 1973, vol. II, pp. 141–2.

14 On the current general state of this question, which is a true *topos* in Heidegger criticism, see my *Introduzione a Heidegger*; also the study by E. Mazzarella, 'Il problema della "Kehre" nel pensiero di M. Heidegger', in *Atti dell'Accademia di Scienze morali e politiche*, vol. XC, 1979.

15 Time, in *Being and Time*, is 'temporalized' or *zeitigt*.

16 See e.g. the first essay in this volume.

Index

~

187